100% GENUINE NO BONES JONES CUSTOMER COMMENTS

D1628594

I am a meat eater first and foremost... (but) man, I was blown away!!! It was awesome!! I have never had vegetarian food satisfy me like that. I can't stop thinking about it!
MIKE WEBB, AUSTIN, TEXAS, USA

Best food on-site! Been coming to Glastonbury for so long now and No Bones Jones is my Number 1 food place.
ORANGE FACE LADY

No Bones' red bean stew is the finest veggie meal I've eaten anywhere, including restaurants.
MICK NAPIER, READING

Had the BEST pre-Rolling Stones bread-and-butter pudding at Glastonbury that you could ever imagine. No Bones Jones are the best!
ANDREW, IPSWICH

In a field full of terrible meaty festival food, this is a shining beacon. THANK YOU!
CHRIS

Best meal all festival. 5-star service.
MOLE

Your food was absolutely fabulous in the Eisteddfod. Bought No Bones Jones food every day!
GWYNETH, NORTH WALES

Your food was amazing. I normally like meat, but I loved it.
DAVE MIDDLETON

The perfect filling for a Tiny Tempah + Elbow sandwich!
AILSA + CHRIS

Amazing food whereby me (vegan) and my gluten-free mate can eat happily together. Thank you!
BEX

No Bones Jones has the best bread and butter pudding in the WORLD. It is the only thing I eat at Glastonbury – MAGIC.
PHIL MICHAEL

As a 'gluten-free' person, eating out is a real chore – you made it a pleasure. Thanks.
JEN

A healthy, balanced meal, bursting with taste.
MICHELLE

Yum – well worth the morning mish across muddy fields. DELICIOUS!
MEG

Never found veggie food so good.
SUZANNE

I had dinner here last night – it was the best thing I've EVER HAD.
JESS

This is so delicious, I come here every year and I'm not a veggie!
MICHELLE, SOMERSET

I don't come for the music, I don't come for the drugs, I don't come for the sex – I come for the bread and butter pudding!! You never disappoint.
SARAH, LONDON

NO BONES JONES
FESTIVAL COOKBOOK

HUGH & JILL JONES
WITH MARK JONES

Hugh & Jill: To our four boys –
Harrison, Frazer, Harvey and Oliver

Mark: To my two sons,
Matthieu and Alexandre

First impression: 2019

The publishers wish to acknowledge the support of
Cyngor Llyfrau Cymru

Cover photograph: Rebecca Bedford
Cover design: Y Lolfa

Photos from authors' own collections unless otherwise stated

© Photos copyright Rebecca Bedford: pp.18 (pans, lentil pour, stew),
23 (spices), 90–1, 93, 95, 99, 100–1, 103, 105, 107, 109, 111, 117,
119, 121, 122–3, 125, 127, 129, 130–1, 133, 135, 137, 145, 147,
151, 153, 155, 156–7, 159, 165, 173

© Photos copyright Iolo Penri: pp.113, 115, 139,
141, 143, 149, 161, 163, 167, 169, 171

Images from Wikimedia Commons used under licence:
https://creativecommons.org/licenses/by-sa/4.0/legalcode

ISBN: 978 1 912631 06 3

Published and printed in Wales
on paper from well-maintained forests by
Y Lolfa Cyf., Talybont, Ceredigion SY24 5HE
website www.ylolfa.com
e-mail ylolfa@ylolfa.com
tel 01970 832 304
fax 832 782

CONTENTS

PREFACE

When Hugh asked me to help him write this book I was absolutely thrilled. I've known Hugh since we were children playing together in the sodden green outdoors of Mid Wales; climbing trees, fishing at the pool up the road, building huts, riding bicycles, sledging, damming brooks, venturing far from home on long walks and indulging all the whims that come naturally to young boys let loose in nature's abundance. So writing a book together struck me as being yet another excellent new project to embark upon together. I'd managed to stay in touch with Hugh for all those years that now stand between us and our childhood, except when he disappeared for a while in the 1980s, travelling and driving a bus for tourists across Turkey, India and Nepal. When he left, he knew little about food or catering, and cared even less. When he came back, he was a man transformed! He seemed to have gone food-mad and enthused at length about the exotic salads, magical spices and fabulous flavours he had discovered in far-flung lands. He seemed to have set his heart on crafting here at home these same delicious, mainly veggie dishes of vibrant colour and fragrance.

This ambition led him to dabble for a while in a restaurant but then he and his wife Jill set up No Bones Jones, a catering outfit which over the next 25 years was to become famous across the country for its hearty, wholesome veggie meals.

Hugh told me that people were now asking for a cookbook to make No Bones Jones food at home, and they thought the time was ripe to share their knowledge of tasty veggie cooking more widely. But they wanted more than a recipe book: they wanted to show where the ideas for their food originally came from and set things properly in context. So here in these pages you will find easy-to-make recipes for summer salads from the Mediterranean, Greek veggie moussaka, Turkish stuffed vegetables, Indian fritters and samosas, Nepalese curries and lentil dishes, starters, main dishes, side dishes, desserts, cakes and breads, and every single one of them is veggie or vegan. And accompanying these recipes is the often amusing story of Hugh's travels, his discovery of new countries and cultures, his determination to get where he wanted to go, and how along the way he stumbled upon the wonderful food that inspired him and fired his and Jill's enthusiasm for the No Bones Jones veggie and vegan cooking that is now yours to discover or re-discover and enjoy at home.

Mark Jones
May 2019

Hugh Jones and Mark Jones

INTRODUCTION

The No Bones Jones Stand at the National Eisteddfod

NO BONES JONES: HOW IT ALL STARTED

I pushed my empty plate away, leaned back in my hard wooden chair, breathed a sigh of contentment and reflected on how much I was going to miss this place: KC's restaurant, where I'd eaten some amazing food and spent wonderful evenings jamming with other musicians. An hour previously, and for the very last time, I'd parked the bus around the back of the Kathmandu Guest House, handed the keys and the *carnet de passage* to my boss, and was just about ready to go home. A tuk-tuk would take me through the bustling, colourful, narrow back streets and I'd say goodbye to this mystical, eclectic city. It was time to move on and I needed a break and a rest.

Hugh right back where it all began: driving an overland bus across Europe and the Indian subcontinent

I'd had an exhausting time as an overland driver travelling between Kathmandu and southern India, covering some 35,000 miles on what looked more like bombed-out airstrip than actual road! Being responsible for the passengers and keeping the old bus going was a mammoth task, drawing on all my skills as an engineer and a social diplomat! Who was more exhausted, me or the bus? We were both totally templed out!

I'd been wandering around Europe and more particularly the East for years, and on my travels I had fallen in love with the honesty, simplicity and sheer deliciousness of the wholesome food I'd eaten along the way. I'd been vegetarian for most of that time and in many of the places I visited, vegetarian food was readily available. This wouldn't be the case back in Britain.

By June 1985 I was safely back in the beautiful rolling hills of Mid Wales. It was harvest time and I could smell freshly cut hay and wild garlic in the hedgerows. The ancient oak trees looked magnificent at dusk and my first pint of real ale tasted wonderful. My mother gave me tea with her delicious home-made *bara brith* and told me my former girlfriend from my schooldays, Jill, was now running a vegetarian/wholefood café. That's interesting, I thought – I'll go and visit.

To cut a long story short, we combined my recollections of the flavours I'd experienced in Turkey, India and Nepal with Jill's extensive knowledge of cooking and bonded over the idea of creating delicious curries and veggie bakes.

First we worked together in the café then ran a restaurant for six years. Since then we've been working the festival circuit. So if you add it all up, it's been over 30 years since we started our journey together, cooking simple, wholesome, delicious food to sell.

IT'S A FAMILY AFFAIR

The business soon became a real family concern because during that time we had four sons – Harrison, Frazer, Harvey and Oliver – who grew up spending their summers hopping from festival to festival, working on the stand and cooking with us from a very young age. Oliver, the youngest, was only three the first time he came along!

Hugh, Harvey, Harrison, Jill, Frazer & Oliver

Back home we always had something freshly baked waiting for the children when they burst through the door after school – they were always hungry! For me, one of the most wonderful times of day is when everyone gets together around the table to eat. For the cook, it's an expression of love for the people they're feeding and an expression of respect for the food they're cooking – well, that's how I see it, anyway.

EMBRACING VEGETARIANISM AND VEGANISM

Things have changed over the last decade or two. Being a vegetarian or a vegan is no longer considered odd. The past five years have seen hugely increased interest in eating more plant-based meals, therefore making vegetarianism more mainstream and no longer a fringe choice.

It's also really important to remember that you don't have to be a vegetarian to eat veggie food! You're not a pigeon, so don't pigeonhole yourself. Eating veggie from time to time may be the first step to becoming a vegetarian, or maybe it won't. It's entirely up to you. Maybe you want to eat more healthily, maybe you want to help save the planet, or maybe you simply want to enjoy a change. Whatever your motivation, the recipes in this book – which have been developed over 25 years and cooked time and time again, so we know they're foolproof – will help you prepare tasty, wholesome veggie dishes at home to enjoy and share with friends and family.

One thing I learned on my travels is that variety is one of the greatest joys of life – and that goes for food too, so it's important to fill your plate with a range of different flavours, carefully selected to blend together harmoniously into a satisfying whole. Although our vegetarian food is crafted to be healthy, that doesn't come at the expense of flavour. Quite the contrary. We want everyone to enjoy not just a healthy meal, but also a very tasty one.

Proof of this is that we've been cited several times in the Good Grub section of the *Glastonbury Festival Survival Guide* – a booklet handed to each festivalgoer with useful advice, a map and suggestions on where to eat. We've also headlined in *The Independent*:

IT'S GASTROBURY! BYE BYE TO THE BOTULISM BURGER, HELLO TO VEGETARIAN CURRY AT NO BONES JONES.

So whether you're trying to go veggie or vegan, or just want to cut down on meat but aren't sure where to start, the recipes in this book should be just the ticket: they're mostly quick, are all straightforward, are guaranteed to be delicious and will help take the focus away from centring your meals around a piece of meat.

OUR GREEN ETHOS

From the outset, and despite the small budget we had to set up our No Bones Jones food stand, very important to us was the emphasis on achieving a low carbon footprint. So when Glastonbury Festival created The Green Trader Gold Award, it was right up our street and gave us something to aim for.

This precious distinction is awarded by Greenpeace, the Soil Association, the Fairtrade Foundation and the Nationwide Caterers Association to just one of the more than 400 food traders on-site – the trader who can best show how, in a variety of ways, they reduce their impact on the environment.

Our efforts were rewarded when we won the Glastonbury Green Trader Gold Award in 2011, but I wanted to go further – so our vehicles now run on bio-diesel and I've invested in a cutting-edge solar-powered system to run our coffee machine and lighting. This has been a great success because when the main power systems fail, our lights stay on!

Also, to keep our carbon footprint small, we do our best to reduce packaging by ordering food supplies – e.g. rice, lentils, beans, gram flour, sunflower seeds, pumpkin seeds, etc. – from a central co-operative in large 20kg sacks. Spices and herbs we source by the kilo and all vegetables are ordered in bulk in returnable crates, from a supplier not far from where the festival is taking place so as to minimise shipment.

Two people were the main influencers in helping me with this approach. The first was my mother who, like all mothers of that era,

Our prized Glastonbury Green Trader Gold Award

Our truck, which runs on bio-diesel

knew how to prepare a nutritious meal from very little and how to make do and mend. It's nothing new to recycle, reuse and repair. People back then had grown up during the war with very little, so their whole '3Rs' approach was not so much a virtue as a necessity, and at the time was simply called good housekeeping.

The other person was a young Nepalese woman in a little shack on the side of the Rajpath, the road leading into Kathmandu, cooking her *dal-bhat* on a dried cow dung-fuelled stove for three rupees. Barefoot she was with her two young children, but nevertheless successfully eking out a humble living. In her hut I was dining in the original 'lean start-up', the antithesis of a modern restaurant and for me far more exciting.

At No Bones Jones we ensure that our operations have the lowest possible environmental impact, meaning that you can enjoy great quality, conscience-clear festival food at its best.

GIVING SOMETHING BACK

The Nepal Earthquake in 2015 brought back to me a flood of memories of my happy times spent in that country. The photographs were devastating and although foreign aid and other help went straight into Kathmandu, some of the poorest surrounding villages were the hardest hit. I had remained in contact with Tony Jones, a retired overland driver still living there. He was focusing on supporting rural Nepal and had sent out a plea on social media for funds. We decided as a family to have a fundraising evening to help. No Bones Jones supplied the Nepalese-style buffet and the guests paid what they thought their evening was worth. Their generosity was such that we raised over £1,500 that night to support the people of rural Nepal.

We've done lots of other charity gigs too. They include fundraisers for various local causes, such as dance nights for the Friends of Montgomery School, where we've booked entertainment like Mike Sanchez's amazing band or the incredible American blues player Brooks Williams, and we've provided the food. We've also been involved with several charity evenings

The Nepal Earthquake fundraiser

in the Town Hall in Montgomery, for example to raise money for the local fast-response vehicle, where we managed to get legendary guitarist Albert Lee and his band to play.

FESTIVAL LIFE

The No Bones Jones stand has for years been a regular feature of festivals like Glastonbury; the Shrewsbury, Chester, Warwick and Beverley Folk Festivals; Wales' National Eisteddfod; Wonderwool; Womad; Colourfest; Clun Green Man Festival; The Green Gathering and many more private and public events. I love doing festivals because of the freedom they offer – reminding me of when I was travelling, moving from site to site rather than just being stuck in one place all the time. Checking the spices and the myriad of things I have to remember to take, and then loading up

Fraz, Harri, Warwick and Sam having a ball on the stand

the van is always a thrill. When we arrive we have 5m of grass, and it's up to us to build a working eatery that will attract festivalgoers. Not only does your food need to be exciting, fresh, modern and colourful, but your stand does too!

Doing festivals is a lot of fun! There are so many unusual and fascinating people around, looking for new sights, sounds, tastes and experiences. At any moment of the day you can end up talking to anyone about anything, just as I did when I was travelling – people seem to be much more open when they're away from their everyday lives. At the same time, it's very hard work. We start at about 8 a.m. and are still going at 11 p.m. – festivals expect their food traders to be open all day, and to have a good variety of dishes on offer. Also, the logistics of the whole thing are tricky – the cardinal sin is to run out of things on the Sunday afternoon! We have about ten people working on the stand, hailing from all over the world: Brits, Australians, Russians, French, Germans – you name it! It's great

The whole Glastonbury team, ready for a big night out after a long day on the No Bones Jones stand!

having that international flavour in the people around you as well as in the food itself.

This isn't a job for everyone – it's very full-on and you have to be good at coming up with quick solutions when things go wrong. You definitely have to be a problem-solver! But we work as a family and the kids have always been involved – I encourage them to build things and make things, and I see how being in that environment has fired their imaginations. And of course at festivals you have the added bonus of being able to sneak off for a little while to see some of the greatest musicians in the world!

FEEDBACK FROM THE PUBLIC

We've been lucky enough over the years to receive an enormous amount of really positive feedback from customers. It's great to know something you've cooked has made people happy. But I think the ultimate endorsement was an email we had from Mike Webb, a confirmed barbecue-loving, carnivorous Texan...

Hi everybody,

I'm a musician from Austin Texas and I was in Bishop's Castle to play at the Gumbo Fest. I should tell you that I am a meat eater first and foremost. I have never felt guilty about it either. After we were done, my wife went over to you all's tent and came back with a plate of food. I had been eating burgers and such. She encouraged me to try some and though I do like meat I really have no problem with veggies. So I took a couple of bites... and man, I was blown away!!! It was awesome!! She went and got me a plate and I ate the whole thing and I felt as fat and happy and satisfied as if I had just eaten a steak dinner with all the trimmings!

I gotta say I didn't eat any meat the rest of that day or the next day! I have never had vegetarian food satisfy me like that. If I had, I would have considered a vegetarian lifestyle quite a bit more seriously. And now I do! I can't believe I'm saying this, but I miss your food! I didn't notice anything on the plate that resembled faux meat or anything like that. I didn't notice any cheese [fake or real]. Truth is, I didn't really know what all there was in it but it was awesome and I can't stop thinking about it!!! Do y'all ever come to the States or do I need to come to the UK for that experience again? Don't get me wrong, we have vegetarian/vegan restaurants and food here, but nothing that ever moved me. I would love to see y'all come to Austin sometime. We have a lot of music festivals here and although Texas is pretty redneck, Austin is a cool town. I think you could do well here. If I could find food like your food here I could cut back on the flesh considerably.

ON THE AIRWAVES

One person who's been unwaveringly enthusiastic about No Bones Jones is Radio Wales presenter Eleri Siôn. One day a BBC Radio researcher came up to our stand at a festival in Cardiff and did a short interview with me about our food. She invited me to appear on the Eleri Siôn afternoon show on Radio Wales and in the heat of the moment I said I'd love to. A few weeks later I was heading by train to Cardiff with my nerves getting the better of me – it's quite something to cook live on air for thousands of listeners! I kept telling myself to relax: it was going to be fine. Thankfully, that first show went well and for several years now I've been a regular on 'Foodie Friday', where I cook and talk to Eleri about the particular veggie dish I'm making that day. They've even run the show live from our stand at the National Eisteddfod, and this year they had me in to do something special on St David's Day – quite a compliment!

Hugh and Eleri Siôn in the BBC studio

An outside broadcast from the No Bones Jones stand

Cooking on the radio is nerve-wracking and there's always the niggling worry that it might all go wrong live on air, but fortunately that hasn't happened so far! Eleri is a lovely person and she's been so supportive – she's even called me the King of the Festival Food Stalls, though I really don't know about that!

THE NO BONES JONES MADE-FROM-SCRATCH QUALITY GUARANTEE

When running a business, you need to have rules, and one of the non-negotiable, rock-solid rules at No Bones Jones is that we will not serve our customers anything we don't eat ourselves or give to our kids. We don't like pre-processed food so we don't sell it. We don't like fizzy drinks so we don't sell them either. It's as simple as that. Everything we prepare is from the simplest of starting ingredients. Also, in order to offer a high-quality product to our customers, we decided from the outset to serve a meal on a plate, not something between two pieces of bread. Our aim was to provide a mixed, nutritious vegetarian meal. This was something most unusual in those early days, but it was what we ourselves wanted to eat. We started with two dishes: lentil stew and chickpea curry with brown rice and salad. In 1995 this was considered *off piste*, but we knew we were on the right track and we've never looked back.

Jill and Hugh Jones, the brains and the brawn behind No Bones Jones!

THANKS

First and foremost, I need to say a huge thank you to my amazing wife, Jill – none of this would have been possible without her. She's not just my left hand, she's my right hand too! With her extensive knowledge of food and cooking, she really compliments my problem-solving abilities on the food stand, and together we've worked hard on these recipes to make them as tasty and as foolproof as we possibly can.

My kids are brilliant – they've always laughed at me and made sure I've been kept down to earth! Thanks so much for all your help over the years, boys.

It's been a privilege to get to work on this project with Mark: my oldest, closest and most-trusted friend. His wit and writing skills have made the whole experience a blast.

I'd like to thank the two photographers who have helped make this book look incredible – Iolo Penri and Rebecca Bedford. They were both great to work with and their photos are fantastic!

I'd also like to thank Geoff Hann of Hann Overland for giving me the opportunity to work for his wonderful travel company. He changed my life forever.

Finally, I want to extend my warmest thanks to Eleri Siôn and Radio Wales, who have been incredibly supportive since I first had the idea of publishing a book.

Hugh Jones
May 2019

1 | MAGIC BUS

The Magic Bus

July 1979, a Saturday night: I'm standing on Platform 3 of Amsterdam Centraal Station with a one-way ticket in my pocket. I'm about to set off into a new world, at least for me. I have no one to meet me the other end, no hotels booked, no cars rented, no maps to consult, no guide book, no compass, no nothing. I don't even know what I'm going to do when I get there! It's a leap into the unknown. Goodbye to routine, goodbye to just about everything I know.

I'm not boarding a train. My ticket is for the Magic Bus, Amsterdam to Athens. It's hot in the station and the people on Platform 3, mostly young couples, shuffle about expectantly. A voice calls out suddenly from behind us, "Those travelling with Magic Bus, follow me." I turn and see a tall, scruffy young man with very long hair, dressed like me in jeans and T-shirt. My heartbeat picks up. My hands are clammy. I'm nervous but I'm really excited too. I follow him out to the rear of the station and there's the bus.

The idea had come to me about a year earlier, when I was in Paris with my brother and his wife, visiting her sister. She'd said, "Come on over, it'll make a change." I'd taken a couple of days off work and while I was there, wandering about doing my tourist thing, I met some Americans in a bar. We got chatting, as you do. When I asked if they were on holiday, they said, "Yeah, we're travelling for three months."

I was genuinely amazed. I thought, how can you do that? I mean, I got two weeks' holiday. In the UK *everybody* got two weeks' holiday, as far as I knew. And these people were travelling for *three whole months*! They were going all over the place, right across Europe. How could this be possible? I admired them, and they opened my eyes to the fact that it *was* possible. You *could* do this, if you wanted to. And suddenly I wanted to! I thought, if they can do it, why can't I?

A job is security. I was trained as an engineer, and the boss said to me on my first day, "You get two weeks' holiday; then, once you've been here for five years, you get two floating days you can take off any time in the year." Well, after talking to those Americans, I got to thinking that the world I was living in was way too small and too narrow. I wanted to step out of it and into another. I wanted to go and do what the Americans were doing. Discover new things. I wanted to build up my confidence. And I was thinking that while I was in the factory turning out bits of diesel engines, these people were travelling, experiencing things, drinking up the wonders of the world. So I'd better do something about it.

I was working for Rolls-Royce in Shrewsbury and I got to thinking that if I could get a job in Europe, then at least I would have made a start. I managed to get a six-month contract with a small engineering company in Zaandam, close to Amsterdam. I also needed to get some money together, so the whole time I was in Holland I didn't go out, and I spent as little money as I could.

After working for six months and saving up as much as I could, I left the company and went to the Magic Bus office on Damrak, the main avenue in the centre of Amsterdam. I bought a one-way ticket from Amsterdam to Athens. It was £33. Magic Buses also went to Istanbul and to Kathmandu, but that was a bit beyond me at the time.

The one to Athens went from Centraal Station. I got there early, ridiculously early. When the scruffy guy with the very long hair called out, I followed him out of the station then round one side of the building to the mythical Magic Bus parked round the back. Now, I know what you're thinking. You're thinking Magic Bus equals Magical Mystery Tour. You're seeing in your mind's eye a multi-coloured, psychedelic, LSD-inspired bus with a sticky-out bonnet and the whole thing spray-painted in gaudy colours with flowers, pictures of the third eye and mountain landscapes, and around it a bunch of happy hippies with beads and beards, long hair, floppy tie-dyed T-shirts, sandals, the lot.

Well... not really. The bus is a fairly ordinary Greek 52-seater, with two very ordinary non-hippie Greek bus drivers. I walk up to the luggage bay. The rucksack on my back is heavy, loaded with most of the supplies I think I'm going to need for the trip: spam, tinned peas, all manner of tinned food. We load up our bags, climb on board, and we're off.

Once I'd packed in my job, I didn't really care what happened. Friends said to me, "What are you going to do?"

"I don't know," I said. "I don't care. I'm just going to do something."

It was exciting. Oh God, it was exciting!

The bus was almost full. A lot of the passengers were teachers who could take time off in the summer. Others were students. I sat on my own and stared out of the window as we left Amsterdam and set off across the flat European landscape. We stopped from time to time for toilets, then rolled on. The trip was long. Very long. We went from Holland through Belgium, then France, to Paris, then down to Italy, through Yugoslavia and on to Athens. At every border between countries a guard would climb onto the bus, walk slowly down the aisle staring at every face, and stamp our passports with an entry visa. This was a bother in the daytime, but if we happened to cross a border in the middle of the night, the guard would shake everyone awake in the dark, shine his torch into sleepy faces then stamp each passport so that we could carry on. Not great. Three nights and three days.

You may be wondering where we showered. That's easy: we didn't. For three nights and three days, nobody washed – not really. Nobody slept much either. It was hot and the bus had no air-conditioning. It may be difficult to imagine what state we were in by the time we entered Athens. After three nights and three days we had the body-odour signature of a twelfth-century Carpathian peasant. Those who took the bus to Istanbul must, on arrival, have resembled the Visigoth barbarians who sacked Rome. And as for those who went all the way to Kathmandu, any locals seeing them disembarking in the Nepalese capital must have reflected on how easily Western Europeans can revert to their Neanderthal roots!

We drove at last into the centre of Athens at about 9 o'clock at night and halted at an ordinary bus stop on a very busy street. I was wondering where I was going to sleep, what I was going to do, what was going to happen. For the last three days (and nights) I'd been in that sort of zombified sluggish trance you get into on long trips. Your intestines pack down, your feet swell up, your body is like a heavy sack. Everything is slow and repetitive. Now, suddenly, we were all turfed out of our familiar little mobile world and a veritable horde of noisy hawkers and all manner of agitated people swooped down upon us. They were shouting into our stunned, bleary faces. "Hey! Good hotel! Good hotel! Come stay in my hotel. Come, come, we have good hotel! Come, come!" Little boxy cars jammed behind the bus were beeping their horns madly. The bus drivers, who wanted to get on, were throwing our bags out of the hold onto the pavement, making a rapidly growing pile. "Good hotel! Good hotel!" the hawkers were shouting. It was all a bit bewildering. But I thought, well, this is it, isn't it? This is what I was looking for. I didn't have a guide book or any kind of information and neither did most of the other ex-passengers, so finally, once we'd rummaged through the bag pile and found our stuff, five of us – two couples and me, who'd met on the bus – huddled together and decided to go off with this one particular hawker chap. We ended up on a hotel roof, with our backpacks, to spend the night in sleeping bags. There was a shower up there, which we queued up for, and toilets, all out in the open air. But it was Athens in July and the night air was warm and gentle.

We were all really hungry so after a while we trooped downstairs and along the street, looking for something to eat. We wandered in front of a restaurant and the chap outside gave us the "Please, welcome, please come in, please come in" routine. We went in and it looked alright – in fact it looked pretty good. Some of the people with me had been to Greece before and they ordered *meze* (dips such as houmous, taramasalata and tzatziki) and Greek salad, with red onions, tomatoes, cucumbers, black olives and feta cheese. All this was brought to our table. I'd never seen any of this stuff before. We also had some sort of grilled lamb. There was bread on the table too, in a basket, and I remember thinking, where's the butter? Then I noticed that the others were dipping their bread into the dressing on the salad, so I did the same and it was fabulous. It was the first time I'd experienced Mediterranean food and the Mediterranean way of eating. I was taking it all in, gulping it all up, and loving it.

The young guy sitting next to me at the table was a photographer. He'd come to Athens to take pictures. "How long are you out here for?" he asked me.

"I don't know," I said. "Maybe three months, maybe longer."

His eyebrows shot up. The people at the table couldn't believe it. They must have been wondering who this guy was, so footloose and fancy free. "Haven't you got something to go back to?" they asked.

"No," I said. "I want to travel. I want to see the world."

2 | GREECE

Grape picking wasn't *all* hard work!

Athens in the daytime was as hot, dry and baking as an oven, and I was the Sunday chicken, plucked and ready to broil. Out in the street the sun scorched my chicken skin, the roasting air seared my chicken innards, and the heat waves pulsing up off the pavement sizzled my tender chicken flesh. From time to time I basted my limbs with suntan lotion and kept on cooking. Then I was a rat, rushing from one sharp, black slab of shade to another. Tight along walls I scurried, then quickly across sun-blasted open spaces I dashed to leap, this time as a fish, into any pool of darkness, through which I swam slowly, savouring the relative cool. In all these different forms I was also a tourist, visiting museums, climbing the hill to the Acropolis, walking the ruins. It was instructive but also wearying.

Every evening I returned to the hotel roof, which I still shared with about ten other Magic Bus survivors, but the whole business was exhausting and after about a week we decided we needed some fresh air.

We took buses and a boat to the island of Naxos, where we lay on the beach. I was no longer a chicken or a rat or a fish. I was a lizard. We swam in the sea. We slept on the beach. This was a lot better than Athens – at least we could breathe! After a few days we scuttled to Santorini. We swam in the sea, we lay on the black volcanic sands. I could breathe, but I was bored, so I left the lizards on the beach and got a boat to Crete, where I decided to get some more culture. I bought a tourist guidebook and a map. I walked round ruins, I took some photos, I went into museums and looked at pots. I took a close look at my map and walked down the Gorge of Samaria to the sea. From there I took a boat to Paleochora where I joined up with a mate and we spent two weeks camping out on the beach. It was the middle of August, life was easy, but I was looking for something, and this wasn't it. We made campfires with driftwood, like you see in the films, and sat on the sand staring into the flames, reflecting on life and wondering what to do next.

I had realised by now that hanging about sunbathing and swimming was not satisfying my thirst for adventure and discovery. I took another look at my map and saw that a ferry went from Heraklion to Alexandria in Egypt. That's for me, I thought. Just what the doctor ordered.

Dreaming of pyramids, I made my way back to Heraklion, and to the ferry office to get my ticket, but they told me the boat didn't sail any more. This was a blow. All my fantasy images of me stepping off the boat in Alexandria, drinking tiny cups of mint tea under palm trees and eating dates by the occasional oasis suddenly evaporated into the thin desert air. Wandering out of the office, feeling deflated and at a loss, with no idea of what to do next, I sat down in a park under some trees and tried to think. I must have looked pretty desperate because after a while a youngish Greek guy came up to me, introduced himself as Dimitri, and asked if I'd like to do some work at a vineyard. As I had nothing else to do, and seeing he was offering food and a place to sleep, I accepted. He told me to sit tight and returned shortly afterwards in an old van. He pulled up, the door flew open and I got in, to find myself packed in with about ten other guys – French, English, all sorts – all in very high spirits. We set off with much creaking and bumping to his vineyard in a village not far away.

I worked there for only three days. I picked grapes, and to do this was given a sort of serrated knife and a couple of buckets. The vines were laid out in rows of fairly low, back-breaking bushes. The bunches of grapes nestled in the centre of the bush and these we cut off at the stem then put into our buckets. When those were full, we hoisted them onto our shoulders, with the metal rings digging into our flesh and, with the sun beating down, carried them up to and emptied them into a trailer at the end of the row. They were for raisins, not wine. At the top of the vine worked a huge, beefy, blue-eyed German guy with long blond hair: Otto. His T-shirt was tight across his broad muscled chest, his large blond head sat on a thick fighter's neck and cords and veins stood out on his monster arms. We took the trailer to him and with huge hands he transferred the grapes into rectangular plastic crates. These he then dipped into a trough of white liquid and two English girls hung out the bunches to dry on wires strung between concrete posts.

Dimitri's father, who was about 65, was a small, rough-skinned, shrivelled-up kind of guy who spent most of his day shuffling around big Otto as he worked, winding him up about the war. He would go on and on at him, really sticking it into him all the time, all day long. It was quite embarrassing. He gave Otto a really hard time. He was like an old black crow picking away at a great white buffalo. I expected Otto at any time to pick the old man up and dunk his head in the magic liquid, just to shut him up, but he never did. He was gruff in a big guy sort of way, but he never got angry. I started thinking after a while that maybe the family had taken him on just so that the old man could pick at him as retribution for grievances past.

We started early while it was still cool, at about 6 o'clock. Dimitri's father would take a break from niggling Otto to drive off in the van at about 9.30. He'd come back at 10 and we had a 15-minute break. We'd eagerly congregate around the back of the van as he pulled down the tailgate and laid out olives, fresh bread and ripe tomatoes. Then he'd flip the top off a large tin can, dip his hand into the watery contents and pull out a huge lump of real, authentic Greek feta, dripping with brine. He placed this on a piece of newspaper and cut it into chunks with a knife. We almost flung ourselves onto this simple but delicious spread, eating standing up, grinning at each other, with tomato juice running down our chins. I remember wolfing down these delights and gazing through the bright shimmering Mediterranean air at the towering mountains all around. This, I thought, is a moment to savour. It was heaven.

At the end of the three days, Dimitri paid us off in cash, in drachmas, and those of us he thought had worked well got shipped off to a pal of his in a nearby vineyard. The people here were much older, well into their eighties, Mama and Papa. When we got there, I realised this place was technologically far more advanced – on account of the fact that they had a donkey, called Marco. While we were picking, George (Papa and Mama's son) would bring Marco down to us and we'd empty our buckets into big baskets slung on his sides, saving our bruised shoulders. We started at 6 o'clock and stopped at midday for lunch. Papa would take us in his van for the short trip into the village nearby where they had a house. Mama would cook us a meal and we'd sit round a big table together. It was cooking from the heart, all fresh food, lots of salads, quiches, omelettes, fresh bread, olive oil, houmous. After the meal we'd go for a siesta out on the wide balcony before returning to the vines for a few more hours when it was cooler. I stayed there two weeks.

Two English guys working with me at Mama and Papa's were making their way back to Britain overland across Europe, having spent six months in a kibbutz in Israel. They were full of great stories about the place, about the communal way of life. This really appealed to me because I didn't want to go back to a British winter, and as it would mean having a roof over my head, I decided then and there to go to a kibbutz myself.

After saying farewell to Mama and Papa I took a boat to Athens, arriving at the port of Piraeus, then caught a bus into the city. I stayed three days in Athena's now familiar furnace and used my Greek drachmas to buy a ticket at a travel agent's for a flight to Ben Gourion airport in Israel. When the time came, I took a bus to the airport and went to El Al's check-in.

The security was amazing. I'd never experienced anything like it. They questioned everybody. They body searched us, they searched our bags, they scrutinised our papers and all our personal belongings. They really grilled us, but in the end they let us through.

When I landed in Tel Aviv, they stamped my passport with an entry visa. It was late evening so I slept in the airport. The next morning I took a bus into the centre of Tel Aviv and went to the tourist office, where they gave me a rudimentary map and directed me to a kibbutz office across the city. On my way there on foot I passed lots of catering vans selling food in the street. I was hungry so I stopped at one that seemed popular with the locals. When my turn came, I looked up at the guy through the open side hatch of the van and, given that I couldn't recognise any of the food on offer, I asked for the same thing that everyone else in front of me seemed to be having. The man gave me a pitta bread with falafel, salad, houmous and dressing. It was delicious and was the first time I'd ever seen falafel. It was also the first time I'd bought Mediterranean food from a street vendor, and what a whole world away it was from the hot dogs I'd bought from carts on the streets of London, with their plastic-looking frankfurters warmed in hot water, their limp bread, soggy onions and dollop of ketchup.

I walked on and eventually found the kibbutz office in a small side street. They said they were looking for people to pick oranges. That suited me – I'd do anything. They pointed to a map on the wall and asked me where I wanted to go. Thoughts of the grey British winter flitted through my mind. "As far south as possible," I said, "where it's warm." So we picked Kibbutz Re'im in the Negev desert. Now as luck would have it, a guy from Kibbutz Re'im was up at the office that day, so after a bit of a wait, I chucked my rucksack in the back of his pick-up truck, clambered into the front seat next to him and off we went, south.

3 | KIBBUTZ RE'IM

Our band – just on the verge of breaking through!

My chauffeur's name was Shimili and he drove us down a long, lonely tarmac road that snaked through a dusty, stone-strewn landscape under a hot, pale sky to Beersheba at the northern end of the Negev desert. Along the way I kept a lookout for the mythical city of Penalyps, which I'd heard of as a young boy while sitting every Sunday morning next to my parents in church. I used to listen with half an ear to the vicar's sermon and sing-song incantations while in fact my mind was more on fishing and football and climbing trees, and other far more interesting boyhood pursuits. One thing the vicar mentioned did, however, fire my imagination, and that was the city of Penalyps. As part of his service, the vicar used to chant regularly in a grave, sonorous voice, "Oh Lord, oh Penalyps," and I could see in my mind's eye the great shining city of Penalyps on a hill in the Holy Land, with golden domes and emerald spires reaching for the heavens. Great bronze doors set in massive stone walls would be heaved open at dawn to the sound of trumpets, admitting kings, merchants and pilgrims, come from far across the ancient world.

Sadly, one day years later, bum on pew, I realised that the vicar was not at all chanting, "Oh Lord, oh Penalyps," but "Oh Lord, open our lips," and my vision of the city on the hill crumbled into the dust.

But gazing through the window of the pick-up truck, I still half expected to catch a fleeting glimpse of it out of the corner of my eye. After all, Israel *is* the land of miracles!

Eventually we arrived at Kibbutz Re'im. Here the desert had been pushed back and trees and grassland had replaced the stones and scrub. The place was surrounded by a fence and featured a pillbox, in the shade of which sat a guard called Amos. He had an Uzi machine gun. All the staff had machine guns. Inside the fence were wooden huts for sleeping, each containing two single beds – army-issue: metal-frame with a bit of an old mattress – and also a communal fridge outside on the porch, and an outside sink where you could clean your teeth. There was also a dining hall, a shower block and a shop. Sprinklers did their best to keep some grassy patches alive between the buildings and an irrigation system ensured that parts of the kibbutz were quite green. There were even some cows!

About 200 people lived on site. Kids had their own dining area and also their own dormitory. They didn't eat or sleep with their parents. In fact, they only saw their parents for two hours a day, from 4 p.m. to 6 p.m. It was socialism that worked, more or less. Most of the people on the kibbutz were Israelis but there were also about 30 foreigners: Germans, Dutch, English, Americans, French – all young. Everybody worked. And quite naturally, along with most of the other foreigners, I was assigned to pick oranges.

The orange groves were about 2 km from the kibbutz and we commuted to work in a trailer pulled behind a tractor. The trailer had wooden bench seats down each side and a canvas top. We rose early every morning and were in the groves by 6 a.m. We finished at 11 a.m. then returned to the kibbutz for lunch in the communal dining hall.

Picking oranges was a simple affair for which we were issued with clippers, a shoulder bag, a steel ladder and a hat. About 24 people went to the groves in the trailers and were split into pairs. Each pair was assigned a big empty wooden crate 2 m long on each side and a daunting 1 m high. This they had to fill before they could go home. The pickers stormed up the trees by means of the ladders, clipped the stalk protruding from the orange and placed said orange in aforementioned shoulder bag. And woe betide anyone caught pulling the orange off its stalk instead of clipping it from its sturdy anchorage, for then it would come to pass that foreman Rocky (not the boxer – another one, much bigger) would come to this person and rain down upon them his mighty wrath, and verily I say unto you that Rocky's wrath was a terrible thing to behold and was known far and wide across the land and unto the very shores of distant seas. When the shoulder bag was full of neatly clipped-from-the-stalk oranges, the picker clambered down the ladder and emptied their harvest into the wooden crate. Once their crate was full they helped the slower people so they could all go home.

I picked oranges for about four months and was then moved into the kitchens, even though I knew next to nothing about cooking. I started off peeling garlic and making falafels. To do this, I mashed up chickpeas, under supervision, and once I had mastered this, I was given the job of frying the chickpea mix. They had to be brown, not burnt. Falafel for 200 people – that's a lot of falafel! The kitchen had an Israeli manager, and I was just doing what I was told. I was peeling vegetables, washing up, cleaning, slicing bread in a machine, general stuff. Cooking chickens. Lots of chickens. We'd bake them in rosemary. No pork, obviously. We prepared potatoes, salads, stuff to go into a cold buffet. For breakfast there were eggs – boiled, poached or scrambled – with toast. Breakfast also included cheeses and olives, tomatoes, turkey slices. None of the food was very interesting. It was all basic mass catering, which is difficult to make exciting. We did, however, make our own mayonnaise in a massive cauldron-like food mixer. I couldn't believe you could make mayonnaise like that – I thought it came in a jar!

Shortly after I started in the kitchen, a new guy was assigned to join us. He was a Russian Jew, ex-Soviet navy, about 55, and everything about him contrasted sharply with the slim, baby-faced youths who were the kibbutz's main occupants. He was short but seemed big because of a hugely out-of-proportion broad chest that merged at some point with a large belly, and this peculiar morphology required him to lean backwards slightly when he walked. On top of this boulder of a torso was perched a large round head, capped with very short grey hair. There was no discernible neck.

The first time we met was in the kitchen, and I was about to start chopping some onions. The door opened and in he came. He was like a supertanker bearing down on me. He grabbed my right hand, crushed it, held on, and stared up at me with unblinking intensity. His big body was right up against me. His big round face was uncomfortably close to mine. I could smell his breath. His milky, pale blue eyes were fixed on mine.

"You Hugh," he informed me gruffly, staring straight into my eyes. "I Yuri, I cook." His gaze didn't shift. He didn't make any attempt to move away or let go of my hand.

"That's good, Yuri," I said, nodding like an idiot.

"I wash up," he said, still staring into my face.

"That's... uh... that's great, Yuri," I said.

"I cook on ship," he said, "big ship, *ochen bolshoi.*"

He was still staring intently into my eyes. His face was still too close to mine but I couldn't move back because he was gripping my hand.

"Little kitchen," he went on. "Very *malen'kiy*, but many men. Must have order in kitchen. I have order in kitchen. You are understanding this, *da?*"

"*Da, da,*" I replied, nodding again, trying to look earnest.

He looked at me doubtfully for a moment then let go of my hand and dropped his gaze.

Actually, Yuri was alright, just a bit overly serious. And true to his word, he *did* cook. But what he really excelled at was washing up! Before I met him, I thought washing up was.... well.... washing up! But Yuri, in his little grey galley buried in the bowels of a great Soviet warship, had turned washing up into an art, a thing of scientific beauty. And as an engineer, I admired that. He washed up with method, precision, discipline, agility, effectiveness and rapidity.

I did my best to learn from him, the two of us standing at the sink, master and apprentice. With time I became quite proficient at it, and although washing up is only washing up, it's nice to be able to do it really well and really fast.

I started my kitchen shift at 8 a.m. and finished around 3 p.m., which left plenty of time for other activities. When an American girl, Michelle, turned up with a guitar, and seeing that I'd always been interested in music and could play the guitar and sing, I asked to borrow it. Michelle liked to play and sing solo, mainly country music. I was more blues and rock 'n' roll, and because there was no entertainment on the kibbutz and I knew a few songs, there were plenty of people who would come and listen. So at night we'd have a few drinks and I'd get the guitar out and we'd have a bit of a sing-song. The main building housed what was laughably called 'the music room', owing to the fact that it contained an old piano and a bit of a drum kit. I met a Dutch guy, Kurt, who was a great boogie-woogie piano player with a fabulous bass figure left-hand rhythm, and Olaf, a German chap, who had actually trained as a drummer and could do paradiddles, press rolls, all manner of rhythmic acrobatics, and he could really get things swinging. So with me singing and playing the guitar, the three of us got together and started a little band. We rehearsed in the music room then, for public performances, we moved our kit into a building called 'The Disco', which in fact was an old bomb shelter. On account of this we called ourselves The Bomb Shelter Blues Band. We played early Elvis, Neil Young and lots of Bob Dylan. What better place than a bomb shelter to sing about peace and love? Word got out and after a while other kibbutzes started asking us to come round and play our music in their bomb shelters too!

Back on the job, mashing my chickpeas, it occurred to me one day that preparing and cooking falafel for 200 people in a kitchen was not so very far removed from turning out bits and pieces for diesel engines in a factory. Admittedly, machine oil is different from olive oil, lathes are different from ovens, and industrial tools are different from kitchen utensils, but I could see that the processes involved in factory work and mass catering were remarkably similar. Had I come full circle? Was I back where I started? Truth be told, I was getting tired of churning out bucketloads of mass-produced, mediocre grub and at the same time I was getting more and more into my music. The band was going great – people loved what we were doing. My voice was getting stronger and my guitar playing was coming on in leaps and bounds. If I wanted to get seriously into the music scene, I couldn't do it here in the desert: I had to go where it was all happening. I had to go where it was buzzing. I had to go to London! I arranged the trip, packed my bag and left the kibbutz with a smile on my face. I was going to be a rock star!

4 | IN THE DRIVING SEAT

In London (left), ready to leave on my first trip for Hann Overland!

It was the early eighties and London was throbbing with music. For a budding rock star like me, this was definitely the right place to be. The trouble was that I didn't like London. I was a young Welshman used to open spaces, green fields, hills and mountains, streams and pools. From the top of the little hill in Wales next to where I lived as a boy, I could gaze out eastwards across a plain that ran uninterrupted in hazy blue flatness right across the Midlands. In London, the furthest I could see was down the road and across the street. The whole place was a giant warren of brick and tarmac.

I was living in a houseshare in Hounslow which, in estate agent-speak, had 'convenient' access to Heathrow Airport. My next-door neighbour said I'd get used to the noise. I didn't. I purchased ear plugs and an acoustic guitar and went out to join a couple of local bands. I also went to as many live music gigs as I could. One of my favourite groups, The 45s, were young and vibrant, playing covers: mainly Beach Boys, Chuck Berry and some Beatles stuff. I listened to bands in pubs, clubs and bars, getting ideas and working on my singing.

At the same time I got a job with London Transport, fixing buses. I'd always been good with mechanical things so the job suited me well enough and put a roof over my head and food on the table. Speaking of which, my cooking back then, such as it was, had a distinctly continental flavour. At a push I could do a sort of quiche, and a Spanish omelette. Most of the time I ate spaghetti hoops in tomato sauce out of a tin, or macaroni cheese, also out of a tin. My speciality, however, was Hungarian goulash – which I made by frying onions in a pot, then adding a tin of baked beans and a tin of minced beef (yes! I ate minced beef from a tin). I stirred this up to stop it sticking, and *voilà*! The printing on the meat tin boasted 'no lumps of fat or gristle'. That's because they'd mushed all the fat and gristle in with the rest. I knew in my heart of hearts that this wasn't great, that cooking could be better, but I just didn't know how to improve. The mass catering I'd done in the kibbutz was of no real help because I'd just been following someone else's orders. I'd never used spices or herbs. I didn't know how to make a béchamel sauce. In fact I didn't know what a béchamel sauce was! But I didn't really care: music was my driver, all the rest was mere practicality, and I ate with the sole intention of not being hungry.

After about 18 months of this I had to face the hard reality that I was getting nowhere, and time was slipping by. My life was boring and I was dissatisfied and unhappy. This wasn't what I wanted. I was looking for adventure and discovery, but what I saw in the day was the inside of a greasy workshop, and in the evening I listened to people in bands striving like me for success, and – again like me – not finding it. The weather was awful, the food was mediocre, the planes over Hounslow were ever more frequent, everyone was doing better than me, especially the bankers, and I was turning into a moaner. I needed to get back on the road.

An ad in the paper saw me applying for a job with a company called Encounter Overland. They were looking for bus drivers. 'Must have mechanical experience', it said. I went for an interview. I could already picture myself in the East, in Kathmandu, in golden temples under a golden sun. It turned out I wasn't the only one. There must have been 200 of us eager candidates, gathered together in a sort of hangar. The ad had a picture of a bloke holding some binoculars, gazing at the horizon: an adventurer out in the wilds, with mountains looming in the distance. Really romantic, I thought. They took us in groups to a very unromantic workshop in Hitchin where we spent the day taking gearboxes to bits. I knew about mechanics so the workshop was a natural environment for me. A guy then turned up in a big 3-ton truck.

"In you jump," he said. "We're going for a drive."

Well, because I'd driven tractors back in Wales, I found this really easy and at the end of the day when they called us in, it turned out I was one of 12 selected for a placement.

They flew the chosen 12 out to Tunisia for a week at a training camp, driving trucks about the place, just to get a feel for the job. The funny thing is that I don't remember much about the driving. What I *do* remember is all the cooking we did.

We didn't have an official chef, so they drew up a roster and two different members of the group were designated to do the cooking each evening. On the day we arrived, when they asked who wanted to go first, I stuck up my hand and got ready to give them my range of prime dishes. It was fantastic. We'd go shopping every day in local markets, buying eggs, meat and veg. On my first turn I made them quiche, on my second they had Spanish omelette. Unfortunately, the shortness of the course and the rigidity of the roster deprived them of the delights of my Hungarian goulash. But looking round those markets, immersed in the scents of herbs and spices, peering at unidentifiable tubers in baskets, and being in that kitchen really ignited something for me. I realised that you could make something taste nice just with simple ingredients, but you had to know how to use spices, you had to know how to develop and blend flavours. I loved everything about it. Way out in a Tunisian desert, driving buses along dirt roads, I'd unexpectedly stumbled upon what I actually wanted to do in life.

As it turned out, when we got home, they said I wasn't on the right list and that they were letting me go. I was devastated, but no way was I giving up. Someone said to me, "Go and see Geoff Hann at Hann Overland – he's great to work for." He was running four or five buses to Kathmandu – not minibuses, real buses. I then realised that it was no good going any further with this unless I'd got a bus licence. So, with my mechanical skills I got a job at Potter's Yard in Welshpool fixing lorries, and while I was there I went to Oswestry and got my bus licence. Now, a bus licence in London was £1,200 – I got mine in Oswestry for £400. I was staying with my parents, which was a bit of a trial, but I needed to lick my wounds and get my confidence back. I was relatively young and I'd never done any international driving, so I thought that before driving to Kathmandu I needed to get some experience driving perhaps a little less far, but still abroad. I went to see a company called Tent Trek and got a summer job driving minibuses from London to the South of France. On my first day they said to me, "You've got a bus licence. Take this great big, massive, unwieldy, 52-seater bus full of passengers to Paris and pick up the main driver there, then drive on down to Canet-Plage."

So, there I am on my own with the bus, in London's Victoria Coach Station. I'd never driven a huge bus abroad, not even through London, never mind all the way to Paris then on to Canet-Plage. I didn't even know where Canet-Plage was, but I did have a brochure: three swimming pools, two discos, it said. So as I said, there I was, and all the passengers were turning up in the station and I was shovelling their cases into the hold, and they were saying, "Oh, we're so looking forward to going to Canet-Plage", and I was saying, "Oh yeah, you know it's got three swimming pools and two discos", like I'd spent half my life there!

I got back in the bus, with about 35 people on board, put the key in the ignition, looked in the mirror at all the trusting faces, and thought, 'Here we go, let's keep it simple and do this bit by bit. Just head for Dover.' I knew I had to go over the Vauxhall Bridge. After that I was looking frantically for signs to Dover. I've never been so wired! Can you imagine getting lost and having to stop the bus and go into a shop to ask for directions, and the shopkeeper coming out onto the pavement and pointing down the road, "Turn left, then right, then straight across the roundabout", and all the faces peering at me through the windows of the bus? Talk about losing credibility! Luckily, it didn't come to that. I somehow managed to get out of south London then down to Dover and onto the ferry just in time. I was sweating, I can tell you.

I drove up and down to the South of France three times, but it wasn't for me. It was great fun, but I wasn't learning anything. So I wrote to Hann Overland and was called in for an interview. I went along and Geoff Hann said he had a job in Turkey starting in April, for six months. It wasn't Kathmandu, but it was a start!

The pay was £70 a week, half into an account for me and the other half held back till I got home and returned the bus. For expenses they gave me trip funds, for which I had to keep accounts. Our passengers ('pax', we called them for short) would fly into Istanbul and I'd pick them up there. I'd drive over from Britain to meet them in an old 25-seater Bedford bus that was plainly more suitable for day-return trips to Bognor Regis than long hauls across Turkey. It was creamy-white, gave quite a comfortable though creaky ride, was right-hand drive (which made overtaking a bit hair-raising), had four random-access forward gears, and no air-conditioning. The engine was reliable but the suspension was a bit dodgy on rough roads.

Once I'd picked up the pax at Istanbul Airport, we'd spend a couple of days locally then set off east across Turkey. I'd book hotels along the way. Because I'd worked in a Dutch factory for six months I could speak some Dutch, and a lot of Turks had been *Gastarbeiter* in Holland and Germany, so they knew some Dutch or German too, and we could communicate. I also had a *Blue Guide To Turkey* with a list of hotels. Really cheap hotels we used. Also, we went visiting when we got to tourist places. As we had no guide, I had to step into the breach as the font of local knowledge, all drawn the night before from the *Blue Guide*, telling them on what date such-and-such a place had been built, stuff like that. It was a bit disorganised, but I made it what it was. We'd start off spending two days in Istanbul looking at places like the Hagia Sophia, me with guidebook in hand. The passengers were of all types and ages. Some especially wanted to see Eastern Turkey. They knew where they were going, they just didn't want to go on their own.

A typical trip would start at Istanbul Airport with me introducing myself and wondering how we were all going to get along. I was getting paid for this, so I wanted to do the job to the best of my abilities and make sure the people had a great time. It was a 15-day bus and steamboat trip. The steamboat took them up the coast to Trabzon in Eastern Turkey, where they found themselves abruptly thrust into a very unfamiliar world and experienced the shock of seeing kids with no legs on little wheeled carts pushing themselves along in the street with a stick in each hand. It was a tough life up there. I found good hotels, and if the water was hot, I'd book the same hotel again for the next group. I learned to count in Turkish, and I learned *sicak su*, which is 'hot water', and *oda* for 'room'. So you'd have *banyolu oda* as 'room with bath'. The passengers paid for their own room and we ate at local eateries. I started to learn a lot about Turkish food. In the morning we'd have breakfast at a café round the corner where you could get an omelette and plenty of yogurt and honey and Turkish coffee and tea. I realised early on that food was key to getting the group together. We had a kitty, and before leaving the hotel I'd ask who'd like to go shopping. There was a baker in every town and a group of passengers would go there or to the market. At about at 11 o'clock we'd stop the bus by the side of the road for a cup of tea. We'd all pile out and I'd produce a gas stove and a kettle. We'd have tea and the local produce they'd bought that morning: fresh bread, jam, biscuits and nuts and honey, and maybe a bag of apples or pears. The shopping for food and the preparing and eating of a meal together bonded the group. We broke bread together. It was fantastic.

We visited some great places and saw some amazing sights together. We passed through Van and visited the Armenian Holy Cross Cathedral, we saw Sumela Monastery, and the fluted minarets of the Madrasa in Erzurum. We went to Kars, which is right on the Russian border. Here there was no asphalt on the roads, just dirt and donkeys and horses and carts. All the men in the streets seemed to be wearing clothes from the 1930s. It was odd – they were quite smart, but everything seemed so old-fashioned. There were no women in sight; they must have been out working in the fields. The shops had no glass in them, just metal shutters that were pulled down with ear-splitting, nerve-jangling screeches in the evening. At dusk, the only light came from the shops – there were no street lamps. So when the shutters screeched down, the whole street was suddenly dark and the entire population then seemed, as if by magic, to disappear, turning the place into a ghost town. I did three trips to Kars. The first time I got there it was wet and the roads were muddy. I went into the police station and got all the passports stamped, then bought a ticket to go up to Ani, the ancient Armenian capital which is 45 km away across a vast plain. I had no idea what to expect – just a pile of ruins, I thought. But Ani is, in fact, a stupendous place. Marco Polo went through Ani, as did all the caravans travelling along the silk road on their way to Shangri La. As we drove towards it, across a great barren plateau along an ancient stone road, we saw its walls rising up in the distance like a lost city. When we eventually got there, we pulled up and walked to the Lion Gate. Two Turkish soldiers at the gate stamped our ticket, took our cameras off us, then walked us around.

Ani was known as the city of 1,001 churches and at its height in the tenth and eleventh centuries was home to 100,000 Christian souls. It sat on many trade routes between East and West and its splendour was unmatched. Behind the city is a deep ravine cut by the River Akhurian and spanned by an ancient high-sided stone bridge. The central section collapsed into the river long ago, but it's easy to imagine caravan trains laden with silk, gold, spices and other precious goods winding their way down toward the water, across the bridge and up the other side. Ani was sacked by the Mongols in 1236 then devastated by an earthquake in 1319. Most of it is in ruins now, grassed over, but in 961 it was the capital of the Armenian kingdom. In its centre, and still standing, is a massive, beautiful Armenian cathedral, completely derelict. Everything is gone out of it, but the building is more or less intact, looking fantastic. It was originally a basilica but its dome is gone now. The doors are gone too, but when you step inside and gaze at the black and brown stones from which it is constructed, the ornate arches, the nave and the chapels to each side, you cannot help but wonder at the sheer power of faith. You may read all the books, look at all the photos, and even see the film, but you have to be standing there, drinking it in, to really get it. I was overwhelmed – I had not been expecting to feel like this. I was humbled.

Standing there, I could feel all around me the silent presence, not of ghosts, but of the past and the people who built this cathedral, this city and this civilisation. Generations of builders, artisans, craftsmen, soldiers, traders, teachers, musicians and merchants. They used to stand here where I now stood, they used to walk through the ruined doors behind me where I had just walked. This was once a bustling city, its streets thronged with people living their lives, laughing and crying, shouting and singing. Their song of life ended long ago. But in the stillness of the cathedral, I fancied I could still hear the faint echo of its last lingering notes. It came home to me then forcefully how we, like the inhabitants of Ani, are simply passing through only for a moment, and will follow them soon enough into the forgotten past. It was a sobering thought that put things into perspective. We turned around and, with our guards, walked back to the bus.

The Citadel, Ani
Citrat, Wikimedia Commons

5 | THE VAN CHICKEN TRIPPERS

Lake Van and the Cathedral of the Holy Cross, Akdamar Island
Evgeny Genkin, Wikimedia Commons

One afternoon I drove the bus with 12 passengers on board into a town in eastern Turkey called Van, which boasts both a lake and a citadel. The lake is vast - about 74 miles across, so you can't see the other side – and Van is (or used to be) a port on its shore. We parked the bus by a huge 15-foot-high wall made of massive stone blocks. Thousands of years ago this was the old harbour wall where the boats used to come in, trading across the lake. But the lake has shrunk over the centuries and the wall is now stranded out of the water. Nowadays, all trade is by truck around the lake, so the wall sits there as solid testimony to a more sedate and planet-friendly way of doing things.

We were staying in the centre of town in a rather basic hotel: two to a room, no en-suite, with toilet and shower down the hall. After a bit of a paddle in the lake we drove into the town centre and I parked the bus behind the hotel. The streets were decked out with banners and flags, and at the desk they told me there was going to be a parade the next day. Since it was now late afternoon and there was no restaurant at the hotel, I told the passengers we could eat that evening at a restaurant I knew on the main street. It was a great place – the best eatery for miles around and always jumping.

Now it so happens that the Turks in Eastern Turkey buy their electricity from the Russians across the border. And the day we were doing our tourist thing in Van, the good folk of Moscow or Vladivostok must have been a bit short of power because the Russians cut off the juice to Van that afternoon. Or perhaps the Turks hadn't paid the bill. Or perhaps a mountain goat nibbled through the cable. Whatever! Suffice to say that the power outage lasted all afternoon, and this was to have dire consequences later on. Really dire.

At 7 p.m., with the power back on, we all assembled outside our basic hotel and sauntered down the main street towards the restaurant. Underfoot was just dirt, not tarmac, and on both sides of the dusty street were little shops whose owners sat outside on low chairs amid piles of wares spilling out from dim interiors. They were selling shoes, kitchenware, cloth, carpets, clothes; all manner of things. There were butchers with meat hanging in the window, and also bakers, and a few little guest houses just two floors high. Already, from halfway up the street, the delicious smell of roasting chickens was wafting towards us, luring us onward; and once we reached our restaurant, we saw in the window rows of delicious-looking chickens going round and round on a rotisserie thing. We trooped inside past an excellent salad bar and a waiter pushed two tables together for us to sit down. We ordered the chicken, obviously. The place was famous for its chicken. What else could we do? What would you have done?

We had salad as a starter, with tomatoes and greens and veggie stuff. The place was packed. The mayor was there with the chief of police and a bunch of other town dignitaries. They were having a great time, with plenty of glasses on the table. As soon as they saw us, they all came over to our table, shaking hands, saying how great it was to see tourists. Really affable. They talked about the big parade through the town the next day and insisted that we absolutely must come along. They were inviting us specially. We nodded and smiled and promised to be there. Everyone was so welcoming, we were really getting a glow in the warmth of the place.

After the salad, we went up to the rotisserie and this chap took down our chickens, pulled them off their skewers, put them on a sort of board and cut them up with a pair of pruning shears, like you'd use on your prize roses! I remember thinking at the time, 'That's not very hygienic, is it?' I thought back to that moment quite a lot over the next few days! Then they brought the board over and plonked it down in the middle of the table, and we all dined in fine style.

We went back to the hotel, looking forward to a good night's sleep, as we had a lot to do the next day. But, at about 3 o'clock in the morning, I was woken up by an awful, frighteningly familiar churning sensation in my guts. You know the feeling: that sweaty, shivery nausea and inner liquefaction that promises to propel you rapidly to the nearest WC and keep you there for a good few hours, at least. The feeling got steadily worse, then suddenly started to get urgent. Something was definitely on the move! I dashed down the corridor and burst into the toilet, honestly not knowing which end was going to see the most action! I'll spare you the details, but it was bad. Really bad.

One by one the others awoke to do the same dash down the corridor. It was dreadful: a total nightmare. One toilet! All the passengers were there with me in the corridor, all except one young, blonde woman who slept on serenely. Her secret? She was a veggie. She hadn't had the chicken! She slept like a baby through it all until her husband, a chicken-eater, shook her awake and told her he was dying. He was a pathologist, so he knew what he was talking about!

By the morning we were looking very dishevelled, like a bunch of the recently undead – except for the veggie woman, who looked great, especially next to the rest of us. I was also worried about not attending the parade we'd been invited to. I didn't want to let the Mayor down, as he seemed like such a nice guy. As I didn't even know where it was, or when, I decided to ask at the desk. So, after a particularly productive spasm, I gingerly made my way down the stairs and found the desk guy drinking a cup of coffee.

"No parade," he said. "Parade kaput. Mayor sick. Police sick. Everyone sick."

I stared at him for a few seconds, taking in the news, then sped back up the stairs just in time.

We couldn't manage any breakfast. We couldn't eat anything – we couldn't even drink anything. We couldn't keep anything down. Most had done the sheets in on their beds. It was terrible. A few of the braver souls, the least affected, managed to drag themselves up the hill and around the citadel. I stayed in my room all day, with nothing to eat or drink, and kept practising my run down the corridor. We started calling ourselves the Van Chicken Trippers!

The next day we got back on the bus and hit the road. I was driving but I still couldn't eat or drink anything. We stopped about 30 miles out of town by the side of the road and rented a boat, quite a large boat, out to a small island called Akdamar, rising out of the lake about 3 km from the shore. The island is home to the amazing tenth-century Armenian Holy Cross Cathedral with its world-famous bas-relief carvings depicting stories from the Bible. Years ago this incredible work of art, now UNESCO World Heritage, was used by Turkish soldiers for target practice and so is riddled with bullet holes.

We kept going, but I'd lost my strength. I could just about sit and drive, but nothing else. I vividly recall driving across this one part of the Anatolian plateau, between Bitlis and a town called Khata, near Nemrut Dağ (Mount Nemrut), a mountain where King Antiochus I, in 62 BC, constructed huge limestone statues of himself, and also lions, eagles and various gods. The statues are seated but their heads have been removed and are now scattered across the mountain top. An absolutely fantastic place. I was driving along at about 7,000 feet across this plateau which is totally devoid of vegetation – no trees or shrubs, just a tarmac road between one town and the next – and I had to keep stopping for my bowels. I stopped the bus, stood up with a toilet roll in my hand and waved it about a bit at the passengers, and said, 'You all know what's going to happen, so could you please stay at the front of the bus so I've got some privacy'. Then I went out to squat down behind the bus on that flat plateau, with Turkish truck drivers honking their horns as they thundered past down the road and saw me with my arse out in the wind. It was terrible. The bus was stopping every five or six miles for someone to go squatting round the back – a real nightmare.

That night we got into Diyarbakir on the River Tigris. The city is surrounded by high walls of black basalt over three miles long and pierced by four gates. The place is fantastic but its charms were lost on me, I was so ill. The next day we went to the ancient ruins of Harran on the Syrian border. In its prime, Harran was a major Assyrian city controlling the trade route to Damascus. I drank something there but still couldn't keep it down. I felt dreadful. Then we drove on to Khata along a road that takes us across the Euphrates, and I was thinking, 'I just have to get some water into me somehow.' So I stopped the bus, walked down the bank, and jumped in the river Euphrates! My poor dehydrated body sucked up the water. When I got back on the bus I asked John, one of the passengers, to pour cold water over me as we went along. We also put some water on a towel and hung it out of the window. The slipstream cooled it down, then I wrapped it round my shoulders. It helped a little. We stayed two days in Khata then drove a long-haul 400 km to Göreme (in the Cappadocia region), and that evening I managed to eat something for the first time in days. I was utterly exhausted, but slowly, very slowly, I started to recover.

What really sticks in my memory, and what really changed my life, was that while I was squatting down behind that damn bus with clouds of grit and dust being thrown at me from passing trucks, in all my embarrassment and with all the turmoil in my guts, I began – for the first time – to find the idea of a vegetarian diet incredibly appealing.

And just to round the story off, I discovered on the way back that the poor mayor of Van had been so ill he'd been taken to hospital, but one of the very first things he did on being discharged was to make damn sure that restaurant was shut down and the owners run out of town.

6 | THE BLIND MAN

Hagia Sophia, Istanbul, Turkey
Navid Serrano, Wikimedia Commons

I loved Istanbul. It was all bustle and commotion, but it didn't have that crushing, suffocating effect of many other cities. There was plenty of space and much to see. As Constantinople, it was the capital of the Byzantine Empire for more than 1,000 years. This is where it happened; this is where the action was. Philosophers, artists, scientists, architects, engineers and builders all came here. And it shows. They built the Hagia Sophia basilica, which is stunning beyond words, especially when you consider it was constructed in a mere five years between 532 and 537 with nothing but muscle power, ingenuity and a lot of faith. Countless mosques and churches are sprinkled all over the city, Christianity alongside Islam, West alongside East. Palaces, avenues and squares bear witness to past opulence, now in faded grandeur.

While waiting for my passengers to arrive at Istanbul Airport, I lodged at a back-packers' hostel in the centre of the city. I had a small first-floor room all to myself. The window afforded a view over the old city and a noticeboard downstairs was covered with a mosaic of scribbled invitations for fellow travellers to share trips up the Black Sea coast, to Europe or the Middle East. Every morning I left the hostel and walked across the park to the ancient horse-racing track where from a kiosk I bought tea (*çay*, pronounced 'chai') and a cheese-and-tomato toastie for breakfast. I stood and munched my toastie with the Hagia Sophia as a backdrop. It was glorious. A moment of fulfilment. I wanted breakfast to last all morning!

Five times a day the muezzin from atop his minaret called the faithful to prayer, but no-one seemed to take much notice. Cafés and kiosks served glasses of *çay*, freshly squeezed orange juice, peppers stuffed with lamb and, of course, the ghastly and ubiquitous elephant's-leg doner kebab. But in the face of the doner, I had a secret weapon: a concealed jar of Colman's mustard, employed to jazz up my kebab and make it vaguely edible. Little restaurants (*lokantalar*) sold small trays of cheap everyday food. But for something special I used to go down to the Galata Bridge and there, tied up to the dock, was a small boat, and on it three guys with a barbecue. One was filleting fresh fish – bream maybe – the second was grilling the fillets, splashing them with oil and lemon juice, and the third slipped the grilled fillets into baguettes and sold them straight off the side of the boat to people waiting on the quay. It was all so simple, but really special. This was lunch.

The Sultan's Topkapi Palace, the Blue Mosque, the ancient water cisterns that lie beneath the city, the Grand Bazaar, the marvellous but slightly scruffy spice market, all these and more we visited in the first three days after I collected the passengers from the airport. I had left the bus in the port of Trabzon on the Black Sea coast, so when the time came for us to leave Istanbul we took taxis to the dock and boarded a 1960s steamer that had seen better days but featured a nice big open top with plenty of room to walk about. We settled in on the upper deck. There were about 15 passengers with me and we cast off and chugged out from the harbour into the Bosphorus. It was busy, as always. Small boats, some tiny, were speeding across from one side to the other between the two halves of the city, dodging huge cargo ships and oil tankers ploughing gigantic straight water furrows parallel to the shore, into or out of the Black Sea.

It was June and the sky was overcast. I leaned on the rusty rail and gazed back at Istanbul's breathtaking, hazy skyline with its minarets and spires. Seagulls were crying overhead. Some, I thought, may have good reason to cry, for under the Ottomans, when the Sultan became disgruntled with one of his wives, he would have her dragged out of the harem, stuffed in a sack, then tossed into the Bosphorus. The seagulls on the Bosphorus are said to be the souls of these unfortunate women. Quicker and cheaper than getting a divorce, I suppose! Selim the Grim was a particularly enthusiastic spouse-drowning sultan, and although the regular sacking of his wives kept him fairly busy, he still found time to dethrone his father, murder his brothers and nephews (much in the manner of Richard III), conquer Egypt and extend the Ottoman empire to Mecca and Medina. He was also called Selim the Resolute, and you'd better believe it! So the next time you're wiping seagull crap off your chair in an outdoor restaurant overlooking the Bosphorus, just remember to thank Selim the Grim.

We passed slowly beneath the mighty bridge that spans the Bosphorus and joins Europe to Asia. This bridge, coincidentally, is topped with aggregate shipped all the way from Criggion Quarry, just ten miles from my home in Wales. Even a tiny nondescript piece of gravel, seemingly not promised to great things, may one day have a rendezvous with destiny in the larger scheme of man's endeavours. Or then again may end up on Aunty Mabel's garden path. You really can never tell.

The trip up the coast was to last three days. On board we slept in shared cabins and although the boat was no rust-bucket, I can't say it was particularly luxurious. Some of the passengers had booked a first-class cabin and with this came the privilege of eating with the captain at the high table. We docked first at Samsun then pushed on to Giresun for another bit of land leave and eventually arrived in the port of Trabzon. The bus was where I had left it, parked in the harbour under the watchful eye of a one-legged port gatekeeper with whom I had an arrangement.

Sumela Monastery, Trabzon, Turkey

Babbsack, Wikimedia Commons

We stayed overnight in Trabzon and visited a very unusual mosque – originally a church – built between 1238 and 1263. Its frescoes, remarkably preserved, relate the story of the Suffering of Job, and the revolting Trial of Painful Boils. In this particular biblical episode God gives Satan permission to test Job's faith and the whole awful process is depicted in agonising detail on the colourful walls of this ancient church.

Leaving Trabzon in the bus the next day, I was anxious to get on with the trip and we drove up an asphalt road towards the Anatolian plateau with the fourth-century Sumela Monastery as our destination. This tortuous, dangerous road runs all the way to Doğubeyazıt (Dogbasket, we used to call it) on the border with Iran, and Iranian lorries were hurtling towards us in the other direction, their horns blaring, carrying all manner of produce for shipment out of Trabzon's port. The road climbs precariously up the sides of mountains with dizzying drops into valleys below. The countryside around is incredibly green and lush due to all the rain on this part of the Black Sea coast, and the folk who live here are known as the People of the Mist. This is where Xenophon and the ten thousand marched on their way to Trabzon, and Jason and the Argonauts, having just sailed through the Bosphorus, popped into the city and are reputed to have hidden the golden fleece somewhere in the vicinity. I can tell you, there's so much history here you can scarcely move without tripping over a bit of it, poking up out of the ground.

The bus was right-hand-drive, of course, being Bedford British, so I was sitting next to the roadside. At one point, still ascending with green countryside all around, we started going around a long sweeping left-hand bend. About halfway round I saw a man standing on my side of the road, the right-hand side, facing me. He was about 70 and his arms were held out towards me, slightly apart, palms heavenward, beseechingly. He had a long white beard and was wearing a brown jacket, saggy Turkish trousers and a white Muslim skullcap. Right away I could see he was blind. A blind beggar straight out of a biblical story, on the side of the road, out in the middle of nowhere. A small girl with dark curly hair and dressed in a colourful skirt, a pullover and brown plastic sandals was playing at his feet.

For some reason, without thinking, I slammed on the brakes and pulled off the road. I don't know why. I'd seen lots of beggars, but he was different – being blind, I suppose. I climbed out of the bus and walked up to him.

"*Selam*", I said. "Hello."

He said something back that I didn't understand, but it didn't really matter. I was looking into his white eyes, his weather-lined face. It was a nice face, a kind face.

"Hang on a sec," I said, "we've got some stuff for you."

I dashed back to the bus, leapt on board all fired up, and went down the aisle asking the passengers for stuff to give him. It was mad, really.

We came up with bread and jam, chocolate, food we'd bought for our picnic, honey. All these things we loaded carefully into his arms, while he nodded and thanked us over and over again. You could tell he was really in need. He was genuine.

From that day on he was 'The Blind Man on the Side of the Road' and I saw him every time that I drove that route, without fail. And I always stopped and we always gave him something. We broke bread with him. We gave him money too, and were richer for it. He always had at least one child with him and always stood in exactly the same spot on the same bend. Even when the skies had opened and the rain was hammering down, he would be there, arms outstretched. I got to rely on him and would ask the passengers in Trabzon to get some things ready to give him. I greeted him each time as a friend. He became a fixture, part of the trip.

Then one day in Trabzon, just like every time at that point in the journey, I asked the passengers to gather together a few things for him. I drove up the road very carefully that day because it was a little misty. We got to the bend, with me looking out for him, getting ready to greet him as usual – looking forward to it, in fact, like meeting an old friend. I started to pull round the bend, and I couldn't believe it. He wasn't there. He wasn't standing there where he always stood. There was no-one there. No man, no child, no nothing.

I stopped the bus, got out, and walked up and down with the traffic thundering by. I looked in the ditch, goodness knows why. I waited for quite a while, hoping he'd turn up. But he didn't. Eventually we drove off, but my heart was heavy.

I never saw him again, the Blind Man on the Side of the Road, but I still think of him, even now, from time to time. How odd that a blind beggar with whom I barely spoke could have left such a vivid mark on me.

7 | KATHMANDU

Bus mechanics' yard, Kathmandu

Landing at Kathmandu Airport was scary. The mountains around it were beautiful but threatening, the runway was short, the Air India plane I'd boarded in Delhi had seen better days, and most of the other passengers looked just as nervous as me. But gosh, it was exciting!

Geoff Hann, my boss, in a sort of baptism of fire, had sent me to Kathmandu, the roof of the world, to pick up one of our old Bedford buses and take it down to Delhi with a fresh load of passengers who would be flying in a couple of days after me. Kathmandu is a wonderful place. It's busy and thriving. It sits at an altitude of 4,600 feet, in a bowl with mountains all around and the surrounding hillsides are terraced for rice paddies. Sacred cows wander the streets and chickens scurry along the side of the road.

I was booked into the Kathmandu Guest House and, once safely on the ground, a two-stroke tuk-tuk took me there in a jiffy, leaving me plenty of time to unpack and settle in. I had a single room upstairs and after playing a few songs on my guitar, I spent a wonderful evening sitting in the incredibly elegant gardens round the back. The next morning I went out through the gates into the street, looking for somewhere to get breakfast. Before I'd gone three paces I was set upon by a group of hawkers crying, "Hash, change, leather jacket, hash, change, leather jacket!" and crowding round me. Little did they know that I had my anti-hawker technique all sorted by then. Tried and tested, it was. Honed to perfection. I immediately grabbed one of the guys, told him I was literally dying to buy a leather jacket from his cousin up the road, and dragged him off in the direction I wanted to go. The others immediately peeled away, looking for another victim, and I strode off with 'leather jacket' in my wake. After a few hundred yards, he began to realize that I had no intention of buying a jacket, leather or otherwise, and he left me in peace. This worked so well that the next morning when I walked out of the guesthouse, the same bunch of hawkers barely gave me a glance before turning away and ignoring me completely!

Some of the main streets were asphalt back then in Kathmandu but most were dirt or mud and the air was unsubtly perfumed with a rough blend of incense, two-stroke engine fumes and cow dung. Many of the shops catered for trekkers and mountaineers and offered second-hand walking gear and climbing equipment that had been up and down the Himalayas countless times. Many of the shops were fitted with wooden shutters that at night were closed by means of steel bars padlocked across the front. Some were open to the street with no glass window. Walking past them that morning I could see tailors at work and people at workbenches fixing all manner of things. The shops were of a precarious, shaky construction, built mainly of brick, and had a shabby air of neglect about them.

Geoff Hann had told me to rendezvous with a certain Bob Wiggins, a seasoned India driver who happened to be in the city at that time. He was supposed to tell me how to get from place to place between Kathmandu and Delhi. All the tricks, all the pitfalls. When I found him, he was sporting a grubby T-shirt, long unkempt hair and the scruffy look of the long-time traveller. The first thing he said to me was, "I've got to show you where to eat." Obviously a man of priorities! He walked me through the Thamel area of town – where all the tourists go, and all the backpackers have their hostels – until we stood outside Narayan's Pie Shop. Facing the front of this shanty of wooden construction, in the dirt street, he raised his arms as in worship.

"This," he announced gravely, in a voice full of wonder, "is the best pie shop in Kathmandu."

It was his Mecca, his shrine. I thought it a bit odd at the time that the only thing that seemed to matter to him was a pie shop, not the city's culture, its history, temples, squares, palaces, mansions or gardens. But he was right: they did make exceedingly good pies. Apple pies, plum pies, cinnamon rolls and some amazing cakes. How come? Well...

It so happened that in the 1970s a lot of Western hippies who were drifting along the Hippie Trail finally washed up in Kabul, the capital of Afghanistan. They made the place their home, not because of the sun-kissed beaches or nightclubs, but for certain exotic agricultural products they could find there cheaply and in abundance. They lived out their happy hippie existence in peace and love for quite a while, and to finance this tranquil lifestyle they discovered that the pies they could bake were well received and much appreciated by the local populace, so this became their speciality.

Their peaceful pie-baking existence was rudely shattered when the Soviet army invaded Afghanistan on Christmas Eve, 1979. The hippies suddenly found themselves in the middle of a war, with tanks roaring down the street and helicopter gunships clattering overhead. They freaked out! And as the war was also disrupting the supply of the exotic agricultural products to which they were so partial, they decided to pack up their meagre belongings and move on. They went to Kathmandu. And what did they do when they got there? They started baking pies again, of course. And they taught the locals that one way to make money off foreign tourists is to give them something to eat that they are familiar with. Give them what they want, they said, and you're on to a winner. The Kathmandu pie business was born.

Narayan's Pie Shop was one of the best. Inside it was fairly gloomy, with Narayan himself sitting behind the counter. There were lots of tables and wicker-back chairs and a couple of fans revolving slowly on the blue ceiling. At the back of the main room was a serving hatch through which nine or ten Nepalese could be observed, toiling away. I loved being able to see the cooking taking place. This wasn't an industrial food chain where everything is shipped in pre-prepared, just chucked in a frier and then shoved out the front. Here people were working together to craft unique dishes. Aside from the pies, you could get an omelette or poached eggs for breakfast, and of course curries and the ubiquitous *dal-bhat* (lentils and rice). They even did veggie burgers with salad! In fact, all the restaurants in Kathmandu prepared and served their own specific food and most were family run. It therefore followed that each dish was entirely unique and the antithesis of the McDonald's experience, which is the same from London to Los Angeles, from Tokyo to Timbuktu. Ordering a Big Mac anywhere on the planet and knowing exactly what you are going to get may be reassuring, but where's the fun in that?

Another of my favourite places in Kathmandu was KC's restaurant, where you could get a great home-made veggie burger. They also did fabulous muesli for breakfast. A lot of backpackers used to hang out at KC's and there was always an open mike with someone playing a guitar – me included. We used to sit around playing Dylan songs and others like 'American Pie', getting all the customers to sing along. There was no television so we had to make our own entertainment. One of my best-loved dishes at KC's, and what really stood out, was their saag aloo, made of spinach and potatoes, with the potatoes cooked in turmeric. This was fabulous: a really authentic delight, and still today one of my very favourite dishes, which I often make. It's simple, quick and packed with flavour.

Nepal is a wonderful, green country. When I drove the Kathmandu-Delhi trip down the Raj path through the mountains and on to the border at Sonauli, it was striking how the landscape changed from the haven of tranquil, beautiful Nepal into India, which was dry and dusty with bad roads and mad traffic, and towns with very little in them on hot, baking plains. I'd go down to the Ganges at Varanasi, then on to Khajuraho with its temples of erotic sculptures, then on to Agra, Jaipur and finally into Delhi. We'd stay a couple of nights at each place, making it a 14-day trip.

In India it was all curry, and bland curry at that. There was nothing sweet. So after a while, I built up a real craving for sugar. It got so desperate that as soon as I got over the border into Nepal I'd stop at a place I knew where they did chocolate brownies they kept in a safe. Not a money safe but the sort of safe my grandmother used to have, before fridges: like a cupboard with a wire mesh front to stop flies getting onto the food. I'd point at this safe and ask for a brownie, and when it was served up, the first bite was just heavenly.

When I got to Delhi, I'd drop the passengers off at the airport and the next day pick up a fresh group who'd just flown in. We would then set off for another trip: maybe back to Kathmandu, maybe round Rajasthan for three weeks, or even down to the south.

One day I found myself in Madras, so quite naturally I thought I'd go out and treat myself to an authentic Madras curry, completely unadulterated by modifications made to suit the British palate. I wanted the real thing, the real deal. I wandered about the city and went into several curry houses and asked for a Madras curry. All I got was a shake of the head.

"You must have a Madras curry," I insisted. "This *is* Madras, right?" They said it didn't exist. They said there was no such thing as a Madras curry in Madras. I felt hoodwinked. I felt cheated. I mean, it's like going to Champagne and asking for a glass of champagne in a fancy French brasserie and the waiter saying he's never heard of it!

Food has to be authentic, it has to be honest. It should not be pretending to be something it isn't. Nothing should be hidden. There should be no trickery: no horse meat in the beef, no pesticides in the pesticide-free organic broccoli, no additives in the additive-free yogurt. We should know what we're eating. Is that too much to ask? And if the cook claims that the dish is from a particular region, then that should be true. Madras curry is fine and you find it all over Britain: chicken madras, lamb madras, vegan madras. It sounds great, but it ain't from Madras.

8 | THE ROOFTOP RESTAURANT

Mysore Palace
Jim Ankan Deka, Wikimedia Commons

There are rare moments in life when you eat something that has a tremendous effect upon you. It is both unexpected and unforgettable. One of those moments for me was on a hotel rooftop in India. I'd been in the country for six months, and after six months in India, from a food perspective, it was all rather mediocre, all rather much of a muchness. There was nothing exciting or new – it was all the same everywhere. The food was bland, particularly the veggie dishes. I had also learned that no matter the type of restaurant – downmarket, upmarket or somewhere in between – looking at the bewilderingly long menu was a waste of time, and instead I'd always say to the waiter, "Can you please bring me something medium hot and vegetarian?" That's all I wanted in the aftermath of the Van chicken incident. No more meat for me, thank you very much! Also, the fact that I was on a meagre daily living allowance of 70 rupees (about £3.50) meant I had to steer clear of expensive restaurants, so I was mostly rubbing shoulders with the poor folk and all we got was lentils cooked with a bit of curry powder, with maybe a few potatoes chucked in to enhance the 'veggie' status. It was alright, but bland.

On this particular occasion I'd been driving all day and was staying the night in Mysore, the city of palaces. I asked at the guesthouse where I was sleeping whether there was a decent place to eat nearby and was directed to a hotel not far away that had a rooftop restaurant. I wandered over in the evening and found the place to be a small family-run hotel, about three storeys high. I climbed the stairs to the roof and, being on my own, sat myself down at a small wooden table. Half a dozen people at other tables were already eating. The waiter came over with the menu and I gave him my standard line about something medium hot and vegetarian. He asked, "Will you eat egg?" I thought about this for a moment then said yes, despite the Van thing. He went away with my order for egg curry that was going to cost me 20 rupees.

I sat there at my table in the open air, surrounded by the sights, sounds and smells of an Indian city, and for a while I watched the fruit bats circling overhead in the warm February air. The waiter brought my plate and put it in front of me with rice, a naan bread and a bottle of water. The dish seemed ordinary enough. The egg had been cut lengthways into four quarters and these lay side by side in a light brown sauce which, given its consistency, looked to be lentil-based. I dipped my fork into the sauce, not expecting anything special, just the usual blandness. I raised my fork, took a taste and... BAM! It was an entirely new sensation. I was stunned. It was like suddenly being submerged in a sort of marvellously fragrant new substance. I could feel taste buds that had been asleep all my life being roughly jerked awake. Nerves that had never had anything to do were suddenly firing on all cylinders! I was experiencing a fullness and richness of flavours that was truly astounding. It was as if all my life I had been eating in a gloomy theatre with a few candles dotted here and there, and now someone had flipped a switch for every spotlight in the house to produce a great blaze of light. I dipped my fork again. By what magic was it possible to produce such a rich, exciting taste that contained within it, perfectly blended and balanced, a whole range of subtle flavours to produce a perfect whole? It was quite simply the most delicious thing I had ever tasted in my life! Somebody in that little downstairs kitchen in that little family-run hotel in that little unknown street really knew their stuff. They knew stuff I was totally unaware of. Gaping at the dish, I realised that the egg had nothing to do with the fantastic taste, so I pushed it to one side. I then got completely absorbed in the sauce, relishing every drop, prolonging the pleasure. How can I describe it? It was like reading a fantastically good book or watching an amazing TV series and enjoying it so much you want to carry on reading or watching, and never reach the end. I wanted this completely new taste experience to go on and on.

I regretfully finished the last tiny scrap from the plate then paid my bill and walked down the stairs into the street below. I was in a state of emotional disarray. I had just had my eyes opened and my senses exposed to a whole new world of taste that I didn't know even existed. Unbeknown to me at the time, this dish would direct me down an entirely new road that would eventually lead to No Bones Jones.

Now I'm sure you can go to a very expensive business school and learn lots of very useful things about creating and running a business. But that day on that rooftop, for the equivalent of £1, I learned something very valuable that would serve me very well later on with No Bones Jones. I learned that if you can surprise your guests at a dinner party, or your customers in a restaurant, by giving them a far more pleasant experience than they expect, then you will probably have a lovely evening or find yourself running a successful restaurant. The aim must therefore always be to meet or, better still, exceed expectations. That's the key.

9 | *DAL-BHAT* ON
THE SIDE OF THE ROAD

Nepalese cook
Nick DeWolf

Between Pokhara and Kathmandu there was a truck stop. It was the only one along that mountainous route through the foothills of the Himalayas, and was strategically placed where the road split and went down into India. There was plenty of room for trucks to pull in and stop. Strung along one side of this stopping place, overlooking the valley, were tiny little shacks with Nepalese women in them, all busy cooking. Every time I took that road in my trusty old Bedford bus, I stopped there and went into the same little shack. It was my favourite – I absolutely loved it. Like all the others, it was constructed of stone, bricks and mud, with a low roof and a wooden door. It was quite dark inside, with a single small window, and it was hot and rather smoky. Underfoot was bare earth. The shack was occupied by a Nepalese woman about 30 years old, with bare feet, a shawl over her hair, a ring through her nose, dark skin, dark eyes and beautiful teeth. Up against one wall was an open fire, over which was a rudimentary chimney. There was a wooden table and some chairs, and generally a few of these would already be taken by truck drivers. There were a couple of kids playing on the floor in a corner. The woman would always smile at me when I came in, showing her beautiful white teeth. I couldn't speak Nepalese, and she knew no English, but I liked to imagine her smile was saying 'Welcome to my humble catering establishment. I hope you enjoy your meal here and leave contented.' Then again, perhaps she smiled because I was a regular, or because I was a foreigner, or perhaps she smiled at everybody who came in – I don't know. But it was a lovely smile.

I felt good in this little shack – I couldn't get enough of it. She only had one dish to serve, so there was no messing about with menus or pondering what to have. She did *dal-bhat*, the traditional Nepalese dish of lentils and rice. It was three Nepalese rupees. I'd also get a chapati, which is flat bread much like a naan. To cook all this she had an animal-dung fire ringed with stones, and on the stones, covering part of the fire, was balanced an upside-down steel bowl. She would put the chapati on this and leave it there while it cooked. She had another pan, aluminium this time, for the lentils, and a third for the rice. I would sit at the table and watch her until my chapati had cooked. She would then ladle a serving of lentils and rice onto a tin plate and bring it over to me with my chapati. I would also get a fork and a glass of *chai* (tea). I loved the way all this meshed together so simply. Three rupees for *dal-bhat* served up by a barefooted woman in a shack halfway up a mountain.

The *dal-bhat* was fine, but it was still only rice and lentils! So why have I never forgotten it? Why did I love that little shack so much? I think it's because it was so obviously the absolute antithesis of the modern world's inhuman corporate agribusiness, our fast-food outlets and today's mass-produced, standardised, sterilised, additive-enriched, over-processed, vacuum-packed, plastic-wrapped, over-marketed garbage. For me, that is epitomised and embodied by the ubiquitous frozen chicken nugget that some fast-food purveyors make from antibiotic-treated, GMO- and

On my way to Kathmandu, after flash floods washed away part of the road

additive-fed chickens using 50% mechanically separated meat. The rest is fat, ground bone, blood vessels, nerve, eyes (?!) and connective tissues, all of which is mashed into a hideous gloop, treated with ammonia, then 'enhanced' with sugar, salt, starch, fillers and binders to make it taste of something. Up in that shack, everything was exactly what it appeared to be. It was simple, good, wholesome, tasty, unadulterated food. And I don't believe we should have to go halfway up a bloody great mountain to get that!

10 | JAIPUR

My bus in front of the Palace of the Winds in Jaipur

We were back in the bus on a crazy slalom that took us from Delhi to Jaipur then on to Agra, with two days' sight-seeing in each. The sun was bleaching out the landscape around us and the roads were as mad as ever. I was gripping the wheel and sweating as usual as we turned off the main thoroughfare up a steepish hillside to visit the famed Amber Fort, a palace just 11 km from Jaipur. My trusty guidebook said this magnificent fortress of red sandstone and white marble was well worth the visit.

I was driving up the hill, aiming for a handy bus park below the fortress and negotiating a particularly tricky bit of potholed track when the door of the bus was yanked open from outside and I was startled to see a small brown pixie of a man jump aboard and hang onto the door frame as we jolted along. A few moments later we parked up in a cloud of red dust and our newcomer introduced himself.

"My name," he said brightly, "is Eugene Pram. I am your guide and I have been expecting you."

He was rather an odd-looking chap, with a strangely youthful brown face, a grey moustache and – very unusually for an Indian – he was wearing a black French beret on his head and had a European-style pipe in his mouth. His English was perfect and he had a clear, pleasant voice.

I was somewhat taken aback. I had no idea we were going to have a guide, but at the same time I was quite relieved, as I'd never been here before and only had my trip notes to go on.

"Fine," I said.

We slogged on foot up the hill to the fortress, where Mr Eugene Pram turned out to be a wonderful guide. He skipped along beside us, herding us this way and that, and we spent the rest of the afternoon drinking copiously from his fountain of knowledge. The Fort is astonishingly beautiful and elaborate, with great halls, lavish gardens, a whole series of spacious courtyards, stunning views over the surrounding countryside and even subterranean passageways. It is exquisite in its opulence.

Construction of the building we see today was begun by the first Maharajah of Jaipur (Raja Man Singh I) in the late sixteenth century, and Mr Eugene Pram showed us around the royal apartments where the Maharajah used to spend his time. These apartments have one peculiar feature, due to the fact that the Maharajah had twelve queens. Each queen had her own living quarters and all of these were adjoining. They had walls, but no ceilings. Along the top of the walls was a catwalk along which the Maharajah would stroll of an evening, looking down into each queen's living quarters, deciding which of the twelve he would favour with his company that night. Each woman sat in the centre of her apartment on a square stone, waiting for him to come to his decision.

Your heart really goes out to the poor man, doesn't it? Just imagine the burden of it all. Every day all this weighty decision-making – it could really bring a chap down. I know plenty of men who wrestle painfully with chronic indecisiveness when it comes to picking beer or lager, rice

Amber Fort, Jaipur
Sidharth.jha, Wikimedia Commons

or pasta, chicken or beef, potatoes or chips! So having to choose between twelve different queens doesn't bear thinking about. And what if his henchmen, to further complicate matters, rotated the ladies around? Like they do in supermarkets, where – just when you think you've got the whole layout clear in your head – they change everything around and the shelf to which you have often made a beeline for vegan noodles now boasts bake-in-the-tin steak and kidney pies and boil-in-the-bag dehydrated chicken livers! So we can sympathize with the Maharajah, but let's not forget that even though he doubtless had difficult choices to make, at least he didn't have to do the shopping!

After showing us around the Fort and stocking us up with new knowledge, Mr Eugene Pram accompanied us as we drove down to the Khetri House Hotel in Jaipur, where we had rooms booked.

That evening the passengers ate at the hotel, but Mr Pram invited me to dine with him at a restaurant in one of Jaipur's many backstreets. To get there, we took an autorickshaw, which conveyed us through dense, vibrant throngs of pedestrians wearing colourful red and yellow turbans, and all around us and criss-crossing before us were countless bicycles, noisy scooters, oxcarts loaded with the produce of hundreds of cottage industries scattered around the city's outskirts, buses with metal bars instead of glass across the windows, and street vendors pushing carts fashioned with two bicycle wheels, and which they upended to produce an instant street-side stall on which were displayed fruits and vegetables of all kinds. It was mayhem, absolute madness – at least to Western eyes.

When we eventually arrived at the restaurant, I paid the driver and we were ushered inside. We sat at a small table and I had a good look around, checking the place out. I was immediately struck by a large printed sign on the wall. 'NO EXTRA GRAVY WILL BE SERVED', it said. I frowned, puzzled. No extra gravy? I mulled this over while tussling with vivid recollections of my mother pouring gravy onto Sunday's spuds from a hideous fish-lipped, flowery china gravy boat which, according to family lore, was an ancient wedding present from an obscure aunt. With a conscious effort, I pushed this unbidden image to one side and got back to the matter at hand. No extra gravy? What could it possibly be, this extra gravy? I mean, Indian restaurants don't serve gravy, so it's obviously impossible – seeing that they haven't served you any gravy to start with – to have any *extra* gravy.

Mr Pram was once again able to enlighten me. The 'gravy' they were referring to was actually their curry sauce: a curry base that every quality catering establishment in India crafts for its own use. This is the precious secret: their own style of gravy for their own style of curry. This is the base from which they derive a range of dishes. I immediately noticed that some of the flavours in this 'gravy' were entirely new to me, yielded by spices with which I was unfamiliar. Curry, I got to thinking, is a lot more complex than I had been led to believe back in my youth, by the Vesta TV adverts of the 1970s.

"Open the packet," the advert instructed, "then add boiling water."

I could clearly picture the small TV screen showing the beautiful couple in their beautiful dining room savouring every mouthful of their wonderful Vesta curry. For me, this was what it was all about, making curry at home. This was all I knew of it: this advert. I remember thinking back then, gazing mesmerized at the vision on the TV screen, that one day

I'd be married like that, I'd have a dining room like, and a beautiful wife like that, and we'd be happy and smiling, making Vesta curry together. It was my vision of the perfect future. They sold me my lifestyle: something exotic. The rice in Vesta curry adverts was always placed in a perfect geometric circle on the plate, then the curry sauce was poured onto the plate in such a fashion that it formed another perfect geometric circle within the circle of rice. And then, to make the TV picture even more enticing, a delicate steam could be seen to be rising from the surface of the curry, and I could easily imagine the exotic aromas emanating from it as the beautiful, smiling wife set the plates down on the table to the sound of Indian music.

For years after that – and this shows how powerful advertising can be – I believed that if the rice and curry sauce were not presented in the circular manner of the Vesta ads, then it wasn't a *proper* curry.

So when and where, you may ask, did I learn to make a *real* curry? Well, when I was on my own up in Kathmandu waiting for a group of passengers to arrive, I needed to watch my budget and had to find cheap accommodation for myself. But once I'd picked the passengers up at the airport, the trip budget could be stretched for me to stay with them at the magnificent Kathmandu Guest House. While there, a bunch of other mainly Western amateur musicians and myself would sing and play guitars in the garden. I also had a harmonica for some of the Bob Dylan songs, and this all went down very well with the audience. Now it so happened that at that time there was a Tibetan chef working in the Guest House kitchens, and he loved the harmonica. He called himself Richard and regularly used to sit outside listening to us playing away. He loved it, especially the harmonica, and we would chat afterwards about music in general and the harmonica in particular. In the end I gave him my harmonica in exchange for some cookery lessons – and funnily enough, that turned out to be one of the best deals I ever made in my life!

He invited me back to the tiny flat where he lived, in the Thamel area of town. The building he took me to had a wooden door giving onto the street and his flat was up a flight of wooden stairs. Once inside, I discovered a main room with dim light coming through a single window, fitted with wooden shutters but no glass. The window looked out across a narrow alley to a building just a couple of yards away on the other side. The room contained a bed, a table and a few chairs. Off to one side was a very small kitchen with a gas bottle on the floor, a sink, a single tap and two gas burner rings on a small work surface.

He said he'd show me how to cook an authentic veggie curry. On one ring he boiled the rice in an aluminium pan and on the other he cooked his one-pot curry in a frying pan. He began by laying out a great many spices, herbs and other ingredients on a tray. Some were freshly ground, others freshly chopped, as necessary, then as he was making the curry he selected the chilli powder, garlic, turmeric, cumin, coriander, ginger, etc. when needed. He also had fresh coconut, lemons, onions and other fresh vegetables. Cooking a superb curry took him about 15 minutes and we then sat at the table and enjoyed it together. This was authentic Nepalese food and it was really good. So it was in that little kitchen in Kathmandu that I saw for the first time a chef craft his 'gravy', the secret base of all good curries. At that time I didn't know what most of the spices were, but I thought, if he can do it, so can I. The thing that he knew, and what I had to learn, was how to balance flavours. This was his secret. You can learn how to do this, but it's tricky and takes lots of practice. A symphony orchestra is made up of many instruments, and for it to sound right, they all have to be in balance. It's no good having the trombones blasting out over the strings, or the oboes drowning out the flutes. If the piccolo has a part to play, we should hear it. The whole thing comes together to produce chords in harmony, but if one chord is wrong then the entire thing is literally discordant. Food is the same. If you add the wrong thing, or too much of some particular thing, the dish doesn't taste right. And the wrong ingredient can easily work against the others. It's all a question of balance.

This is what I started learning with my pal Richard in his kitchen in Kathmandu. From then on, I really paid attention to how dishes were prepared and how flavours were blended and balanced. In short, I started to take cooking seriously.

11 | HOME AND A NEW BEGINNING

Jill (now my wife) in front of the Castle Kitchen café

I'd been away for years, living out of a bag, and I began to yearn for some structure in my life. I told Geoff Hann at Overland that I'd had enough and I returned to the mountains and valleys of Wales. I caught up with some old friends – including my former girlfriend, who I married and we started a family. My new wife had opened and was running a vegetarian café in Montgomery called the Castle Kitchen. As you can imagine, this was a really groundbreaking concept in the area at that time. I started making vegetarian food with her. We later moved on to open a restaurant in Newtown and went through a succession of chefs, from whom I learned how to make great lemon tart, how to prepare sauces, and also many tricks of the trade such as how to be fast in a kitchen, how to be organised, how to prep properly so that everything is ready when required, how to work tidily, how to organise fridges and how to make sure that everything needed is all together in the same place. It was interesting – fascinating, even – but I found that my work at the restaurant encroached increasingly on my family life, so I decided to take some time out and find a new direction in life.

Out of the blue I got a call from a butcher I knew in Hereford. He wanted me to join him and do some cooking. He said he'd keep me busy all summer. I jumped at it.

Our first assignment was a one-day agricultural show outside Hereford. We had to get there early. The butcher had a van with a small trailer hitched up behind, inside which there was just about enough room for two people to move around without too much treading on toes. A gas oven and a grill had been squeezed in and a number of shelves were located under the side-opening hatch. A few cupboards were scattered about haphazardly here and there, in just the right place to bang your head. When show day arrived, we loaded the van with trays from his shop then drove to the showground, where we parked up. We lit the oven and grill, sorted out our napkins, plastic cups and bags of frozen baps, then stacked up some meat, ready for the oven.

"You can't have pork without apple sauce," said the butcher, while rummaging about in the back of the van. I expected him to bring out a wooden crate full of nice juicy apples, and I could already see myself spending a happy hour peeling a load of Bramleys. But when he turned around, instead of apples, I saw he was holding a big plastic bag with 'Dried apple sauce' printed diagonally across the front in bright green. He promptly chopped the top off the bag and poured the contents into a plastic bucket. He filled the bucket with water and stirred it up with a long-handled spoon. "There's the apple sauce," he said.

I stared at the bucket, thinking it reminded me of something. Suddenly it struck me: wallpaper paste! That's exactly what it looked like. Wallpaper paste in a bucket, ready to go up on the wall in the new baby's bedroom.

Now that we had our apple sauce, we started shoving pieces of pork shoulder and leg into the oven. We also got the bacon out, ready to go, and I set about prying open some pre-sliced frozen baps. Time was getting on. Ours was the only food on the showground and people were already queuing up by 11 o'clock!

We carved up the meat as soon as it was done, slapped a couple of slices into each bap, ladled on a dollop of our apple-flavoured wallpaper paste, and handed it out through the hatch as fast as we could to the sea of heads outside. There were a lot of people there that day and by one o'clock I couldn't shut the till, there was so much money in it!

I didn't have a bap myself as I'd brought my own veggie lunch with me, and although I didn't have time to eat it, it got me wondering as to what any vegetarians would be doing on that field that day, with nothing to eat save bacon baps and pork baps with rehydrated dehydrated apple sauce.

Soon after that I landed another event-related job with an ethnic crafts company, and found myself loading stuff from the back of their shop into a large van and heading for the Urdd Youth Eisteddfod in Crickhowell.

When we got there, I was almost overwhelmed by the pure Welsh beauty of the Eisteddfod's location in the heart of the Brecon Beacons National Park, surrounded by picture-postcard green mountains. The site where we parked up was in fact an arboretum with magnificent mature trees dotted here and there across a huge expanse of the greenest grass you could ever hope to see. It seems so ordinary to locals but, when you've been abroad for years, Welsh grass seems so green you can almost imagine it's been painted. A marquee and several stands and stalls were already set up waiting for us on our arrival. There were four of us in the team: two company men, a girl they'd hired to help out and me. We set about organising our elaborate set of stalls, assembling something akin to a mini department store, then unloaded the van, unpacked the boxes of clothes, diaphanous shawls, trinkets, jewellery, joss sticks – you know the sort of thing, mostly Indian – and set each item in its allocated place so that everything was ready for sale. The whole process took eight hours. Eight hours to set up – it was crazy! I was put to work on the till, and had also been appointed Head of Security, responsible for checking that people going into the changing rooms didn't walk out with five sets of our clothes on under their own.

The Eisteddfod was a six-day event, which was a bit of a problem for me in that I was short of cash and didn't want to be buying food for myself every day and spending a lot of money. I'd therefore brought with me a twin-burner gas stove, a pan, some lentils, a couple of tins of tomatoes, seasoning, onions, potatoes, carrots, garlic and some dried herbs, with the intention of doing some cooking. Once we'd finished setting up our department store, I therefore set about making a fine one-pot lentil stew, which I looked forward to enjoying every evening.

Everything went as planned for a couple of days, then something happened that I had not anticipated. The others on the stand were getting weary of eating sandwiches all the time and began gazing longingly at my lentil stew. In no time at all they were tucking in and I had to make more, then more still. I was feeding the entire crew with lentil stew and everybody was loving it. In fact, they said they liked it more than any of the food available on the site.

By the end of the Eisteddfod I was still loving my lentil stew but I'd had more than enough of ethnic crafts. In fact, I'd been having serious doubts about ethnic crafts ever since I bumped into an Australian couple in Greece. The girl told me she was working a summer job in a Greek craft shop in Rhodes, selling leather goods – mainly bags and purses. Her Greek boss, Stelios, used to say, "When the cruise ships come in with the American tourists, when they come into the shop and look at the leather stuff, you must tell them that my grandmother – tell them Stelios's granny, she makes these things up in the mountains."

You can just picture her, can't you? Eking out a meagre existence in a gloomy stone hovel on a barren hillside by the side of a lonely track. Her window's weeds, her thinning grey hair tied severely in a bun, her crooked back and her arthritic fingers painfully stitching these wonderfully crafted bags, lovingly caressing the leather tanned from the lambs she raises tenderly herself on the slopes of the treacherous mountain that has been the family's home for generations.

No matter that in actual fact all the goods Stelios sells are churned out of a factory on the outskirts of Athens, and no matter that his granny in fact drives a brand new Mercedes and hasn't been up a mountain in her life. 'Granny' means authenticity, wholesomeness, warmth, love, and respect for natural things. 'Granny' is the opposite of 'cold', 'industrial'. It's got to be good, because your granny makes it. It stands to reason. The odd thing about commerce is that the customers *want* to believe the granny thing, the traditional thing. Even when faced with an obvious con. Even when reading a 'Made in China' sticker on the foot of a 'Hand-made-in-Greece' statue of Achilles, or buying *foie gras de canard* that is in fact, on careful inspection, labelled '100% pure pork'.

On the last day of the Eisteddfod, the girl working with me on the stand went off at lunchtime to get herself something to eat. She came back late after about forty minutes, explaining that she'd queued up for twenty minutes for a veggie burger.

I stared at her for a moment while I took in what she'd said. Twenty minutes to get a veggie burger! Things started whirring in my head. She queued twenty minutes to get a veggie burger! Lights flashed, something went 'Ping!' Everything suddenly came together in my own personal Eureka moment: my knowledge of spices gained in the East; my commitment to great vegetarian food; my kitchen savvy gained from the chefs in the restaurant; the almost complete unavailability of decent vegetarian food at festivals; the simple lentil stew I'd made, which everybody loved. All went critical mass in my head and steam was probably coming out of my ears!

As soon as I got some time away from the stand, I walked around the site, looking at what was on offer. How many food stands were there, who was busy, who wasn't busy, who was buying, and most importantly of all: would I be able to fit in? There were three or four meat trailers and a sandwich van. That was it. There were a lot of people on that site and they all wanted something good to eat. Not all of them wanted burgers and chips. Not all of them wanted meat in a bap. Not all of them wanted a sandwich. Some, I thought, surely wanted something else.

12 | GLASTONBURY

The team with our coveted Glastonbury Green Trader Gold Award!

Glastonbury Festival – or, more officially, The Glastonbury Festival of Contemporary Performing Arts – is the most iconic, almost mythical music festival in Britain, if not the world. It is the peak, the Everest, the Mecca, the Shangri-La for successful world musicians. Top billing at Glastonbury is reserved for global giants, past and present: those who have reached the absolute summit of their art and can draw fans in their tens or even hundreds of thousands.

The festival takes place on a farm – Worthy Farm – like Woodstock on Yasgur's farm, but unlike that archetypal festival, it is held nearly every year and from start to finish lasts five days. The farm's cows are pushed aside and innumerable tents, marquees, trucks, trailers and stalls take their place. Glastonbury is an ephemeral city that waxes and wanes, ebbs and flows like life itself. It comes into being through the coalescence of a vast horde. It throbs briefly with its own vibrant intensity before dying and dissipating, only to be reborn a year later.

As it is for artists, so it is for festival caterers, who on the festival circuit talk often about one day going to Glastonbury, imagining what it would be like to set up there, to be part of it. Glastonbury is a dream for caterers, a Siren calling to us, beckoning to us. But not many make it to that most fabled of places. Caterers who want to trade at Glastonbury must apply well in advance, with details of previous festivals attended, pictures of their stand and a description of the type of food provided. Then they wait anxiously for acceptance. I myself applied for four consecutive years before I was successful.

It was June 2000 and I arrived at the site three days before the public at the traders' gate, where I submitted my ticket and in return obtained a sticker for my windscreen, a wristband and my traders' health & safety information pack. I drove through the gate and on down a narrow lane in a state of emotional riot, thinking, 'I'm here! I'm actually at Glastonbury! This is really happening!' I was totally euphoric. I was gripping the wheel hard with both hands as I went down the sloping, muddy lane. As I rounded a corner I suddenly saw before me, laid out across the valley, a vast city of marquees, tents, constructions of all sorts, vehicles, a kaleidoscope of colours, flags flying proudly on long poles and people come from near and far to take part in a momentous event.

I went past the world-famous Pyramid Stage, shining silver, and was stopped by a Festival Marshall. He checked my pitch number then walked me to a sort of circular corral, where he handed me over to a Market Manager who showed me my pitch. Glastonbury was clearly a smooth, well-oiled machine in operation. I was impressed. The corral was reserved for about 30 traders, who were set up around the perimeter with fencing in between to fill any gaps. There was a kebab place, a soup kitchen, a hairdresser's, clothes stands, a barber's, an ethnic crafts place, an Australian steak bar, all sorts. The centre of the corral was reserved for pitching tents, where we slept.

Two people I'd hired to help me were already there waiting for me and we immediately set about unloading the van and trailer and putting up our stand, which was a small marquee with a cooking area at the back and a serving area at the front with a *bain-marie* to keep things warm. I only had a 3 m pitch so it was a bit of a squeeze, but we managed somehow to fit everything in. I set up my hobs, got out my saucepans and put my colourful array of spices in a row, standing to attention like dutiful soldiers ready for action. Later that evening my wife arrived with our two teenage sons. They erected their tents and helped me finish the stand. The next morning I set my two sons the task of scavenging discarded pallets from around the site and building some basic furniture to go out the front of the stand for customers to sit on. I was testing their recycling and woodwork skills! The forecast was dry, the sun was shining and everything was going as planned. It felt good.

The atmosphere all around was electric with excitement, the very air full of tingling anticipation. I'd seen it on TV, I'd read about it, I'd seen the pictures – but to actually be here, to be part of it, was incredible. A gas inspector and a health & hygiene inspector came round and issued me with a green card: permission to trade. This was really happening, and I was eager to get cooking.

The public wasn't arriving for another couple of days but hundreds of traders were already on site – busy setting up their stalls, preparing their wares – and they all needed to eat.

I got started as soon as possible. I had one rule in my head: keep it simple, don't try to be all things to all men. There's a huge temptation to overcomplicate the menu, to be resisted at all costs. My Authentic Nepalese Chickpea & Spinach Curry was a definite, as was my Puerto Rican Red Bean Stew. I also needed my Broccoli, Stilton & Mushroom Bake; my Vegetable Fritters; my Indian Tomato Relish and my Chilli Jam. The forecast was good, so a big, rocking salad bar was an absolute must. I knew I could maintain this all day, thereby avoiding the cardinal sin of running out of something halfway through the day and missing four hours of brisk trade. My policy is that the last plate of food must be as good as the first and I had to be able to achieve this, which is not so easy when dealing with fresh products that need to be sourced every day. I'd brought 20kg sacks of lentils, beans and chickpeas with me, and tins of organic coconut milk, but for fresh produce I took my trusty lightweight wheelbarrow (nicknamed 'the old boneshaker') to the on-site market, where lorries were parked up, full of the fresh veg and salad stuff I needed. I walked up and down inside the truck with the veg man, choosing from big trays of wonderful fresh produce to load up my wheelbarrow with carrots, cabbage, Spanish onions, cucumbers, endives, green salad, mushrooms, red and yellow peppers, green beans, vine tomatoes, broccoli, fresh chillis, mint, coriander, garlic and ginger. Fantastic!

I soon started to get that special festival feeling, where the outside world almost ceases to exist, pre-festival life seems far away and most familiar things are gone. You are in another world – on another planet. It's wonderful!

The public arrived and everything took off. We opened every day at 9 a.m. for veggie breakfast, serving Vegetable Fritters with Indian Tomato Relish. Then for the rest of the day we switched to Puerto Rican Red Bean Stew; Authentic Nepalese Chickpea & Spinach Curry; Stilton, Broccoli and Mushroom Bake; Brown Rice & Green Lentils; Spicy Ruby Slaw; Mint & Apple Pasta Salad; Vegetable Fritters; and heaps of green and endive salads – all served with lashings of home-made Chilli Jam.

Glastonbury is also the biggest accidental food fair in the world, with more than 400 food stands to choose from that year. We stayed open all day, also serving coffee and tea, but no soft drinks – no big-name fizzy drinks. My policy has always been to avoid corporate things, using only wholesome produce, unprocessed raw products bought wholesale to be crafted into our own dishes. I eat our food myself, and feed my family with it. Basically, if I can't make it, I don't sell it.

At Glastonbury, once inside the festival area, you are at liberty to wander around to see anything you like on any of the stages. About 100,000 people attended Glastonbury 2000, plus all the traders and staff. And Glastonbury is not only music. There is also circus, theatre, dance and cabaret. In fact, everywhere there is a bewildering variety of acts and shows that will satisfy even the most demanding festivalgoer.

One evening when I took the old bone-shaker to fetch more fresh produce from the lorries in the central market, the veg man said he'd got 12 boxes of Jersey Royals and that he'd cut me a deal. Each box was 5kg. I said I'd take the lot, all 60kg. You'll think I was bonkers, but my mind was flitting back to a book I'd read called *101 Things To Do With A Potato*!!!! I loaded my newly acquired treasures into my barrow, wheeled them back to my stand and over the next four days I sold the lot in one form or another for breakfast, lunch and evening meal. I drew on my knowledge to craft those salad potatoes into a whole range of delicious dishes. We all went spud mad and everybody loved them.

Another day on my way back from the market I went past a bakery where they were selling loaves of yesterday's bread for a discount. Into the bone-shaker they went. I trundled back to the stand and started making bread-and-butter pudding and, to go with it, our special sticky toffee sauce. The wonderful recipe for this sauce was handed down to me by my grandmother, who, according to family legend, as a nurse during World War I had acquired it from a chef at the Paris Ritz. Granny Jones's Sticky Toffee Bread & Butter Pudding is still a firm favourite at festivals – although she may not be around any more, we still love her pud.

The next evening there arrived at the stand a rather flamboyant chap of about 35 called Pete. He was wearing an old Afghan coat, white jeans, a pink feather boa round his neck and a floppy cream hat over long blond hair. He queued up, peered at the food on display and explained that he would dearly love a plate of curry but had no money. He was, on the other hand, ready to sing for his supper! A special sort of song.

"Tibetan throat singing?" I said. "Never heard of it."

"It's like Mongolian Khoomii," he explained.

This quite honestly didn't enlighten me much, but we struck a deal that he would sing and I would listen, and if I thought he deserved a plate of curry then that's what he'd get. He stood to one side of the queue, took a deep breath and – "YAAAOOOOHHHHOOOOHHWWWOOOHHHYYYO OOWWWHHH". There came out of this skinny little guy in a floppy hat the most amazing sound I'd ever heard from a human throat. It was like two or more voices in one, with a steady deep throbbing bass note, above which floated varied pitches, creating a rich kaleidoscope of sounds.

"OOOOHHHHWWWWYYYOOOOHHHWWWUUUUUWWWHHHH OOYYOOO", he went on, while the people in the queue stared at him transfixed. For about two minutes he sang on, seemingly without drawing breath, and throughout it all was painted on his face a beatific expression of peace and serenity. He got his free plate of curry and while he ate it, he told me about his throat-singing studies in a Tibetan monastery and how this chanting of the monks is part of their ceremonies.

You won't get this sort of thing on the high street outside a standard eatery, but it's exactly the magical sort of thing that happens at festivals.

Glastonbury 2000 saw David Bowie as final-night top billing and no way was I going to miss the Thin White Duke. So when the time came, I abandoned my hobs and went into the main arena to watch and listen. Late in the night he finally came on stage, accompanied by some amazing musicians, a sore throat and a Veronica Lake haircut. He seemed to like festivals. He'd already been at Glastonbury in '71 and his album *Space Oddity* concludes with the hippie-dreaming 'Memories of a Free Festival'. At Glastonbury 2000 I didn't see any Venusians, tall or short, but when he hit the perfect high note in 'Life on Mars', a great wave of ecstasy swept through the heaving crowd, reminding me that 'Satori must be something just the same'.

Now, I may not have been with Henry V on Saint Crispin's Day, I was not at Woodstock in '69, and neither was I in Berlin when the wall came down in '89, but I *was* at millennial year Glastonbury to see David Bowie live up to the legend. And to misquote Shakespeare:

And gentlemen in England now abed
Shall think themselves accursed they
Were not here and hold their tongues
Whilst any speaks that was with us
Upon this day at Glastonbury.

I returned to the No Bones Jones stand and we sat for hours talking about how great David Bowie had been, and about the festival in general and how much we had enjoyed it. I noticed that the sky was getting brighter and that dawn was breaking. We opened up for breakfast – our last shift – then started packing up for the trip home. We'd had a fabulous festival, seen things never imagined, listened to some great music, served a lot of food to a lot of customers and we were now coming away happy. Someone once said to me that you can only enjoy your festival, or indeed your life, if you enjoy your food. That may be true. I know it is for me.

RECIPES

"One of the nicest things about life
is the way we must regularly stop
whatever it is we are doing and devote
our attention entirely to eating delicious
food with good friends and family."

SALADS

CHICKPEA & CHIVE SALAD

VEGAN **GF** SERVES 4 | PREP TIME: 15 MINS | COOKING TIME: NONE

The standard French dressing below is the one we use on most of our salads at festivals. Instead of chickpeas you could use cooked brown rice or quinoa.

SALAD

1 x 400g can chickpeas – drained (or 1 can of any other beans you prefer)

½ red onion – peeled and sliced finely

4 fresh tomatoes – diced finely

¼ cucumber – diced finely

1 yellow pepper – sliced finely

1 bunch parsley – chopped finely (leaves only)

1 bunch chives – chopped finely

DRESSING

2 tbsp lemon juice

6 tbsp olive oil

1 tsp Dijon mustard (optional)

1 clove of garlic – chopped finely

salt and freshly ground black pepper

1. Mix dressing ingredients together, stirring thoroughly.

2. Mix all the salad ingredients together in a suitable serving bowl.

3. Add dressing and mix together just before serving.

GREEK SALAD

GF SERVES 4 | PREP TIME: 10 MINS | COOKING TIME: NONE

This is my version of the beautiful fresh salads I first ate on my first trip to Greece.

SALAD

1 firm lettuce

½ cucumber

4 large vine tomatoes

½ small red onion

20 black or green olives

200g feta cheese

DRESSING

2 tbsp fresh lemon juice

1 clove of garlic – crushed

2 tsp dried oregano

5 tbsp olive oil

salt and freshly ground black pepper

1 Wash and chop the lettuce into bite-size pieces. Chop tomatoes & cucumber chunkily. Peel and finely slice onion. Toss all of this together in a suitable serving bowl.

2 Put all the dressing ingredients into a small bowl. Stir thoroughly.

3 Chop olives and cheese into bite-size pieces.

4 Just before serving, pour dressing over salad to generously coat everything and top with feta and olives.

MINT & APPLE PASTA SALAD

VEGAN   SERVES 4 | PREP TIME: 15 MINS | COOKING TIME: NONE

A good way to use up leftover pasta. Children love it.

225g cooked pasta

4 tbsp olive oil

1 tbsp agave syrup (or any other syrup)

3 tsp mint sauce

1 lemon – juiced

2 chopped apples – sprinkled with juice from the lemon

20 black grapes – sliced in half

4 sticks of celery – sliced thinly

small handful of fresh chopped mint leaves

salt and freshly ground black pepper

1   Make the dressing by stirring together the olive oil, remaining lemon juice, syrup and mint sauce. Season to taste.

2   Add apples, grapes, celery and mint.

3   Pour everything over the pasta and stir well. Season to taste.

SPICY RUBY SLAW

VEGAN **GF** SERVES 4 | PREP TIME: 15 MINS | COOKING TIME: NONE

Everybody loves coleslaw! If we take it off the salad bar at No Bones Jones, someone always wants it back. We like a bit of zing in our food, so we add our Green Spicy Dressing (see p.126).

200g white cabbage – finely sliced

200g red cabbage – finely sliced

2 eating apples – sliced

2 carrots – peeled & grated

3 sticks of celery – chopped

6 tbsp vegan mayonnaise (or use a good quality non-vegan one)

2 tbsp Green Spicy Dressing (optional)

1 Put all the veg and the apples into a large bowl and mix together thoroughly.

2 Mix 2 tbsp of Green Spicy Dressing with the mayonnaise – or more according to your taste for spicy things!

3 Just before serving, add the mayonnaise dressing to the veg and mix thoroughly again.

SIDES

BROWN RICE & GREEN LENTILS

VEGAN **GF** SERVES 4 | PREP TIME: 10 MINS | COOKING TIME: 35 MINS

This is so simple, so inexpensive, so delicious and so versatile. It's also a great source of fibre and protein! I make extra and then use it as the filling for my Stuffed Vegetables (see p.152).

---

2 tbsp olive oil

1 onion – chopped

¼ cinnamon stick

4 cardamom pods

1 cup brown rice – washed & drained

1 cup green lentils – washed & drained

1 Fry the onion, cinnamon stick and cardamom pods in the olive oil over a medium heat for 5 mins (in a saucepan big enough to also hold the rice & lentils later).

2 Add the rice, lentils and 4 cups of water. Stir together, bring to the boil, then turn down and cook over a low heat with a lid on for about 30 mins.

3 When all the water has been absorbed, take off the heat and leave for 3 mins with the lid on.

> **VARIATION**
> When cooking the onion, you could also add chopped **celery and carrots**.

CHANNA DAL

VEGAN **GF** SERVES 4 | PREP TIME: 20 MINS | COOKING TIME: 50 MINS

Yellow split peas have great flavour and create a thicker sauce – super delicious and a great source of fibre and protein!

150g yellow split peas

3 tbsp vegetable oil

1 onion

2 sticks of celery

2 red chillis – 1 chopped, 1 sliced

2 tsp mustard seeds

1 tsp ground turmeric

2 tsp ground coriander

2 tsp cumin seeds

6 cardamom pods

½ cinnamon stick

2 bay leaves

2 cloves of garlic – chopped

2cm piece of ginger – peeled and finely chopped

1 tbsp tomato puree

½ tin coconut milk

2 handfuls fresh spinach

1 handful fresh coriander – chopped

salt and freshly ground black pepper

1 Soak yellow split peas in cold water for 1 hour.

2 Chop onion and celery into small dice.

3 Heat oil over a medium heat in a saucepan big enough to eventually contain all the other ingredients. Add mustard seeds. When they start to pop, add cumin seeds, bay leaves, cardamom pods and cinnamon stick.

4 Stir together, adding garlic, ginger and the chopped chilli. Fry for 1 minute, stirring continuously, then add onion, celery, coriander and turmeric.

5 Drain the split peas and add to the pan. Give everything a good stir.

6 Pour in 750ml boiling water, tomato puree and coconut milk. Cover and allow to simmer gently for 40 mins. Stir from time to time until split peas are soft.

7 Add spinach, fresh coriander and salt and pepper to taste. Cook for 5 more mins.

8 Taste and adjust seasoning if necessary. Garnish with the sliced chilli.

FRENCH BEANS – GLOM STYLE

VEGAN **GF**   SERVES 4 | PREP TIME: 5 MINS | COOKING TIME: 10 MINS

Calling the dressing GLOM helps me remember what to put in it! Delicious served with a main course, or leave to cool and add to a salad.

250g French beans – washed and with stalk end cut off

DRESSING

Garlic: 1 clove – crushed

Lemon: juice of ½ a lemon

Olive oil: 3 tbsp

Mustard: (Dijon) 1 tsp

1   Boil beans until cooked to your liking (8–10 mins for me, depending on size), then drain thoroughly.

2   Put all the dressing ingredients into a jar, screw on the lid and shake well.

3   Pour over your cooked beans whilst still warm.

FRENCH BEANS WITH ROASTED TOMATOES

VEGAN | GF | SERVES 4 | PREP TIME: 10 MINS | COOKING TIME: 45 MINS

My take on a dish called *fasolia* that I ate frequently in Turkey. A delicious accompaniment with many main courses, and can be served hot or cold.

250g French beans – washed and with stalk end cut off

6 large tomatoes – cut in half horizontally

1 whole garlic bulb – cut in half horizontally

2 stems of rosemary – finely chop leaves (discard stems)

olive oil

pinch of sugar

salt and freshly ground black pepper

1 Place tomatoes cut-side up in a roasting tin. Sprinkle with olive oil, salt, pepper, sugar and rosemary. Roast at 170°C for about 45 mins.

2 For the last 20 mins, place both halves of the garlic bulb cut-side down in with the tomatoes. This is easy to burn, so check after 15 mins.

3 When cooked, squeeze garlic cloves out of skin and mix with the cooked tomatoes.

4 Boil beans until cooked to your liking (8– 10 mins for me, depending on size). Drain thoroughly then mix with tomatoes, garlic and a bit more olive oil.

NO BONES JONES
VEGETABLE SAMOSAS

VEGAN SERVES 4 | PREP TIME: 40 MINS
COOKING TIME: 10 MINS (DEEP FRYING) / 20 MINS (BAKING)

Serve as a delicious snack or starter with our Chilli Jam (see p.124) or Green Spicy Dressing (see p.126).

PASTRY

280g plain flour

½ tsp salt

2 tbsp vegetable oil

150ml cold water

1 tbsp cumin seeds

FILLING

3 large potatoes – peeled and diced

1 onion – peeled and chopped finely

vegetable oil

2 cloves of garlic – crushed

3cm cube of fresh ginger – chopped finely

½ tsp ground turmeric

1 tsp ground cumin

1 tsp ground coriander

2 handfuls of fresh spinach – chopped

salt and freshly ground black pepper

1. Preheat oven to 170°C.

2. Roast cumin seeds on baking tray in oven for 4 mins.

3. Put all pastry ingredients in a bowl and mix either by hand or with a food mixer until the dough comes together in a soft ball.

4. Wrap and leave in fridge for 20 mins.

5. Preheat oven to 180°C, unless you intend to deep fry the samosas.

6. Cook diced potatoes in boiling water until just tender (about 8–10 mins). Take care not to overcook. Then drain.

7. Fry onion in 2 tbsp oil on a medium heat until soft.

8. Add garlic and ginger and cook for a further minute, stirring constantly to prevent sticking.

9. Add the spices and cook for another minute, still stirring. Take it off the heat, add spinach and potatoes, season to taste and mix together. Leave out to cool (about 20 mins).

10. Flour work surface, roll out pastry and cut into circles about the size of a saucer. Place filling in the middle and close pastry around it, using cold water to glue edges together. We use an inexpensive samosa press, but you can do it by hand. Carry on until all used up.

11. Deep fry to cook until golden brown (about 8 mins) OR brush with vegetable oil and bake in the oven until golden (about 20 mins).

OUR FAMILY LOAF OF BREAD

VEGAN PREP TIME: 20 MINS, BUT WITH WAIT TIME IN BETWEEN
COOKING TIME: 40 MINS

This recipe makes one large loaf – made every day by Jill. If you are out most of the day, start the loaf as soon as you come home. It's a rhythm with easy steps, not an arduous task. To this standard loaf you can add sun-dried tomatoes, olives, chopped rosemary, walnuts or change the flour for all white. If you use all wholemeal flour, it will have a much heavier texture. Use a large mug as a measure.

---

1 mug of a wholemeal bread flour of your choice (I like granary or seeded ones)

2 mugs of white bread flour

1 handful of seeds – sunflower, pumpkin or any other you prefer

2 tsp active dried yeast

½ tsp sugar

1 tsp salt (you may prefer more)

1 mug water (body temperature)

2 tbsp olive oil

1. Put everything in a food mixer fitted with a dough hook and mix for 8–10 mins. (Or you can do this by hand.) As some flours absorb more water than others, check after 5 mins that everything has come together into a soft dough. If not, add 1 tbsp more water.

2. Leave dough in the bowl, covered with cling film, to rise for approx. 45–60 mins. It MUST double in size, but this will take a different amount of time depending on how warm the kitchen is.

3. Flour a 2lb loaf tin or a solid-bottom medium to large cake tin.

4. Take the risen dough out of the bowl and knock out the air, stretching and rolling it up for about 2 mins.

5. Place in prepared tin and sprinkle top with flour, slash a few times across the top with a sharp knife, then cover with the same film and leave to rise again until doubled in size (approx. 45 mins again). (It must double in size, so be patient.)

6. Preheat oven to 210°C.

7. Bake for 40 mins. Remove from oven, turn loaf out of tin and return back upside down directly on the oven shelf for 5 mins to crisp up.

8. Try to let it cool before slicing off a crusty piece of deliciousness!

ROASTED TOMATOES WITH GARLIC, ROSEMARY & OLIVE OIL

VEGAN **GF** SERVES 4 | PREP TIME: 10 MINS | COOKING TIME: 45 MINS

I serve this with our Fresh Pasta (see p.140) & No Bones Jones Pesto (see p.128).

8 large tomatoes – cut in half horizontally

1 whole bulb of garlic – also cut in half horizontally

3 stems of rosemary – finely chop the leaves (discard stems)

olive oil

pinch of sugar

salt and freshly ground black pepper

1 Place cut tomatoes in a roasting tin, sprinkle with olive oil, salt, pepper, sugar and rosemary. Roast at 160°C for about 45 mins.

2 For the last 15 mins, place both halves of the garlic bulb in with the tomatoes, cut-side down, until just soft. The garlic burns easily, so check after 15 mins.

3 When it is cooked, squeeze garlic out of skins and stir in with the tomatoes.

SAAG ALOO

VEGAN **GF** SERVES 4 | PREP TIME: 15 MINS | COOKING TIME: 25 MINS

I've always loved this dish. When I eat it, I'm taken straight back to KC's restaurant in Kathmandu. I use whole cumin and fenugreek seeds because the flavour is better (in which case you'll need a pestle and mortar or an electric spice grinder), but you can use powder and still get a good result. Top tip: any left over makes a great filling for the Vegetable Samosas (see p.110).

---

4 large potatoes – peeled & quartered

1 tsp turmeric

4 tsp cumin seeds

½ tsp fenugreek seeds

vegetable oil

1 onion – peeled and thinly sliced

thumb-size piece of fresh ginger – peeled & finely chopped

150ml coconut milk

5 cubes of frozen spinach

2 tsp black mustard seeds

3 cloves of garlic – peeled & crushed

300g cherry tomatoes – de-stalked

salt and freshly ground black pepper

1   Preheat oven to 160°C.

2   Add potatoes to boiling water with turmeric. Simmer gently for 12 mins – do not overcook! – then drain.

3   Stir cumin and fenugreek seeds in a dry frying pan over a medium heat for 3 mins, until you can smell the beautiful fragrance. Take off the heat and grind with a pestle and mortar or electric spice grinder.

4   Using the same frying pan, gently fry onion and ginger in 1 tbsp vegetable oil over a low heat for approx. 10 mins. Add spice mix and stir.

5   Add coconut milk and spinach and cook gently together, adding seasoning to taste (1 rounded tsp of salt and a good grind of black pepper for me).

6   Heat 2 tbsp of vegetable oil in a small saucepan. Add mustard seeds, wait until they pop, remove from heat and add garlic. Put back on the heat and cook them together, stirring constantly. They burn easily so watch carefully.

7   Pour onto onion/spinach mixture. Place potatoes in an ovenproof dish, pour everything over the top and mix together gently. Put in the oven for 20 mins.

8   Whilst it's cooking, heat 1 tsp of vegetable oil in the same frying pan and roll the cherry tomatoes around in it for a couple of minutes until they just soften. Ladle them onto the top of the dish when you take it out of the oven.

TURMERIC & COCONUT ROASTED CAULIFLOWER

 VEGAN **GF** SERVES 4 | PREP TIME: 5 MINS | COOKING TIME: 15 MINS

A delicious side dish to go with almost anything.

---

1 large cauliflower – broken into florets

4 tbsp olive oil

2 cloves of garlic – crushed

3cm cube of fresh ginger – peeled and chopped small

2 tbsp cider vinegar

1 tsp ground turmeric

3 tbsp coconut milk

1 tsp soft brown sugar

salt and freshly ground black pepper

1. Preheat oven to 180°C.

2. Mix the cauliflower with 2 tbsp olive oil and spread on a baking tray. Roast in oven for 15 mins, until tender but not too soft.

3. Fry the garlic and ginger in 2 tbsp olive oil on a gentle heat for 3 mins.

4. Take off the heat and add cider vinegar, turmeric, coconut milk and brown sugar. Stir all together and season to taste, then pour over the cooked cauliflower.

VEGETABLE FRITTERS

VEGAN **GF** SERVES 4 | PREP TIME: 10 MINS | COOKING TIME: 6 MINS

I found various versions of this crispy snack all over India, but I particularly remember the ones in Mysore being utterly delicious. Everybody loves a bit of something crunchy on their plate. They are delicious served with Chilli Jam (see p.124) and salad as a starter.

80g onion – sliced

80g broccoli head – chopped into small pieces

150g gram flour (chickpea flour) – sieved

1 tsp GF baking powder – sieved

1 tsp salt and a good grind of black pepper

2 tsp fennel seeds

vegetable oil

1 Mix together the gram flour, baking powder, salt and pepper and fennel seeds.

2 Add 160ml water and whisk to make a smooth batter. Add the onion and broccoli and stir to evenly coat everything in batter.

3 Heat oil (about 6cm deep) in a deep fat fryer or wok on a medium/high heat for about 5 mins. Test the temperature by pouring a little of the batter mixture in – if it crisps up and floats to the surface quite quickly, the oil is hot enough.

4 Drop in tablespoonfuls of the batter mix, taking care not to get splashed by the hot oil – don't drop it from very high!. NB Don't cook more than three or four at once as this will lower the temperature of the oil.

5 Turn the fritters over after about 3 mins to cook on the other side. Cook for another 3 mins, then take out of the oil and drain on kitchen paper. Cut one open to check they are cooked through properly.

SAUCES

CHILLI JAM

 VEGAN **GF** PREP TIME: 20 MINS | COOKING TIME: 35 MINS

An accompaniment to so many dishes, and a firm favourite on the festival circuit. The delicious sweet and sour yin/yang taste is what we all love about this very versatile sauce, and a little jar of it makes a great gift.

If you want it to be thicker and more jam-like, just cook it longer at the boiling stage and it will thicken more. Stir from time to time, but be careful – at some point it will start to catch/burn on the bottom!

For this recipe you will need a large saucepan so it doesn't boil over – it's very messy if it does!

500ml cider vinegar

500g granulated sugar

1 red pepper – de-seeded and chopped

10 red chillies – de-stalked

thumb-sized piece of fresh ginger – peeled

2 cloves of garlic – peeled

salt and freshly ground black pepper

1 tsp ground cayenne (optional)

1. Put red pepper, chillies, ginger and garlic into a food processor and blitz for a minute or so. If you don't have a food processor, then chop as small as possible with a knife.

2. Pour the vinegar into a large saucepan over medium heat for 5 mins, then add all of the sugar. Take off the heat and stir from time to time to dissolve the sugar.

3. Put pan back on the heat, add blitzed veg and bring to the boil. Cook for 30 mins, boiling vigorously.

4. Add salt and pepper. Taste and if not spicy enough for you, stir in a teaspoon of cayenne powder. Take off the heat and allow to cool a little.

5. Pour carefully into clean jars – makes approx. 3 1lb jars or more smaller jars.

GREEN SPICY DRESSING

VEGAN **GF** SERVES 4 | PREP TIME: 10 MINS | COOKING TIME: NONE

This makes more Green Spicy Dressing than you need, but it will keep in a jar in the fridge for a week as long as you make sure it is covered with a thin layer of olive oil to keep the air out. I add it to all sorts of food to give a fresh spicy kick. Our sons eat it as a relish on anything! Used in our Spicy Ruby Slaw (see p.98).

50g fresh mint – leaves only

50g fresh coriander

5 green chillies – de-stalked

½ a thumb-size piece of ginger – peeled & chopped finely

2 tbsp olive oil

1 Place everything in a food processor and blend to a spicy, chunky paste.

INDIAN TOMATO RELISH

VEGAN **GF** SERVES 4 | PREP TIME: 5 MINS | COOKING TIME: NONE

Although this is very simple to put together from store cupboard ingredients, it is a good way to train your palate and connect your brain to your tongue. So make this and try to balance the flavours of sweet, sour, salt, bitter and spice. This is a lesson to be taken forward into everything you cook.

As with everything, use good-quality ingredients. This is delicious served as an accompaniment to nut roast, veggie fritters, a cooked breakfast or fried food that needs that counter balance.

500ml passata

2 tbsp mango chutney

1 tsp salt

1 tsp ground black pepper

1 tbsp sugar

1 tsp chilli powder

1 Stir everything but the chilli together thoroughly.

2 Balance the first five ingredients, then add chilli according to your taste.

NO BONES JONES PESTO

VEGAN GF SERVES 4 | PREP TIME: 10 MINS | COOKING TIME: NONE

I keep the sauce vegan, adding grated parmesan only when serving. Freeze in small batches or keep in the fridge, sealed under a thin layer of olive oil.

200g basil – leaves only

90g pumpkin seeds

250ml olive oil

3 or 4 cloves of garlic

salt and black pepper

1   Toast the pumpkin seeds in a dry frying pan over a medium heat until golden, then leave to cool.

2   Blend the seeds with all the other ingredients in a food processor until quite smooth.

VEGETARIAN GRAVY

VEGAN SERVES 4 | PREP TIME: 10 MINS | COOKING TIME: 30 MINS

Gravy is something that vegetarians often miss. Freeze any left over in an ice-cube tray – very handy for adding to any casserole to enrich it a little.

---

1 small red onion – chopped

6 mushrooms – chopped

3 cloves of garlic – chopped

2 sticks of celery – chopped

3 tbsp olive oil

2 bay leaves

3 stalks of fresh thyme

2 tbsp of plain flour

1 vegetable stock cube

2 tbsp port (optional)

3 tbsp soya sauce (or tamari)

1 tsp miso paste

black pepper

1   Fry the onion, mushrooms, garlic and celery in the olive oil over a medium heat, stirring from time to time, until golden brown.

2   Add bay leaves, thyme and seived flour. Stir thoroughly to avoid any lumps of flour.

3   Dissolve stock cube in 500ml of boiling water.

4   Bit by bit whilst stirring, add vegetable stock, port, soya sauce, miso paste and a good grind of black pepper.

5   Stir all together and taste to check seasoning. Allow to simmer gently for about 20 mins.

6   If you wish to have a smooth gravy, strain through a sieve, pressing down with a spoon to extract as much flavour as possible.

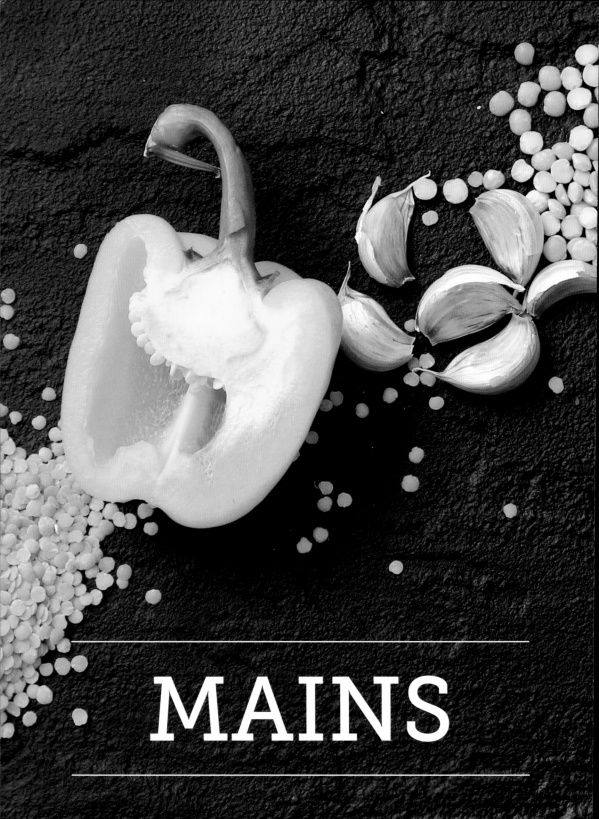

MAINS

AUTHENTIC NEPALESE CHICKPEA & SPINACH CURRY

VEGAN GF SERVES 4 | PREP TIME: 15 MINS | COOKING TIME: 25 MINS

Delicious, healthy and easy to make. A sensational dish to make from your store cupboard. I first came across a simple version of this at a truck stop on the Rajpath – the mountainous road that takes you into Kathmandu. I'll never forget how humble, simple, yet delicious it tasted. It is now a permanent feature on our stand and firm favourite with festivalgoers. It's delicious garnished with our Chilli Jam (see p.124).

---

1 tbsp ground cumin

1 tbsp ground coriander

½ tbsp ground turmeric

300g red split lentils

4 tbsp vegetable oil

6 cloves of garlic – finely chopped

2 tsp black mustard seeds

1 x 400ml can of coconut milk

1 tsp salt and ½ tsp black pepper

1 tsp sugar

1 tsp ground cayenne – or more, as you like

1 x 400g can of chickpeas – drained (or 50g of dried chickpeas, cooked as directed on the packet)

80g fresh spinach – washed and chopped

1. Mix together the cumin, coriander and turmeric.

2. In a saucepan, add the spice mix to 1 litre of water and bring to the boil.

3. Stir the lentils in, turn down to a gentle simmer and cover with a lid. Cook for about 15 mins, stirring from time to time, until the lentils are soft. Remove from the heat.

4. Heat the oil in a small thick-bottomed saucepan over a high heat. When the oil is hot, add the mustard seeds. When they're popping, remove from heat.

5. Working quickly, add the garlic, swishing the pan from side to side OFF THE HEAT for about 20 seconds. It is easy to burn the garlic, so take care. Pour onto the lentil mix and stir in.

6. Add the coconut milk, cayenne powder, salt, pepper and sugar. Give it a good stir, and taste to check the seasoning.

7. Add the chickpeas and spinach and bring to a gentle simmer for 5 mins.

BROCCOLI, STILTON & MUSHROOM BAKE

GF | SERVES 4 | PREP TIME: 20 MINS | COOKING TIME: 20 MINS

I normally serve this with a lovely mixed green salad, and often garnish it with our Chilli Jam (see p.124) – strangely, Stilton and Chilli Jam are an amazing combination!

750g new potatoes – halved if large

2 tbsp olive oil

1 large onion – chopped

2 cloves of garlic – chopped

150g chestnut mushrooms – chopped

400g broccoli – broken into florets

100g Stilton cheese – roughly crumbled

75g cheddar cheese – grated

75ml single cream

1. Preheat the oven to 170°C.

2. Wash and boil the potatoes until just tender (about 15 mins).

3. Steam the broccoli over the potato pan, for just 5 mins.

4. Fry onion, garlic and mushrooms together in the olive oil over a medium heat for 8 mins, stirring from time to time.

5. Take off the heat and add the Stilton, stirring in to melt. Then add the cream.

6. Drain potatoes and mix everything together in an ovenproof dish. Sprinkle the cheddar over the top and put in the oven until hot and bubbly (about 20 mins).

BROCCOLI &
WELSH CHEDDAR SOUFFLE

SERVES 4 | PREP TIME: 40 MINS | COOKING TIME: 40 MINS

Yes, you can cook a soufflé! Follow these easy steps and wow your friends!
NB You will need a straight-sided ovenproof dish no less than 10cm tall, which can hold approx. 1 litre, and a baking tin the dish will fit into to create a *bain-marie*.

450g fresh broccoli

25g butter

25g plain flour

150ml milk

75g grated Welsh cheddar cheese – grated

½ tsp grated nutmeg

1 tsp English mustard

4 large eggs – yolk and white separated

2 large pinches of salt

a couple of grinds of black pepper

1 Preheat the oven to 180°C.

2 Steam the broccoli until soft (about 10 mins). Mash roughly with a fork and leave to cool.

3 Heat the milk gently in a pan over medium heat – do not let it boil.

4 Melt the butter in a saucepan. Add flour and cook together over a medium heat, stirring in the hot milk gradually to make a thick sauce. Cook gently, stirring constantly, for 4 mins.

5 Take off the heat and add 50g cheese, mustard and nutmeg. Taste and season.

6 Transfer sauce into a larger bowl and fold in broccoli and egg yolks. Mix together and leave to cool.

7 In a clean bowl, whisk egg whites to stiff peaks, then carefully fold into the broccoli mix.

8 Grease the ovenproof dish with a little butter. Pour in the broccoli mix and sprinkle the remaining cheese on the top.

9 Boil the kettle. Place the dish in the baking tin and place both on oven shelf. Pour boiling water into the tin to come to approx. 5cm up the side of the dish, to create a *bain-marie*.

10 Cook for 40 mins until well risen and golden brown. Take care not to spill hot water on yourself when removing from oven. Serve immediately.

1

3

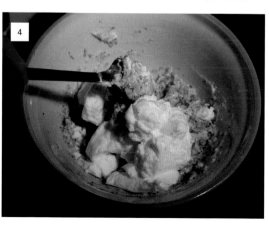
4

CRISPY AUBERGINE & FONDANT POTATO STACKS WITH ROASTED VEG

VEGAN **GF** SERVES 4 | PREP TIME: 30 MINS | COOKING TIME: 20 MINS

A favourite for us at home, and a delicious dish for a dinner party. The photo shows it served with the turmeric sauce used on the Turmeric & Coconut Roasted Cauliflower (see p.118).

---

3 parsnips – peeled and chopped chunkily

2 red peppers – deseeded and chopped

1 sweet potato – peeled and chopped chunkily

3 sprigs of thyme or rosemary

300g vine cherry tomatoes

2 large baking potatoes – peeled

2 tbsp olive oil

500ml vegetable stock

2 aubergines

2 tbsp polenta flour

30g chives – chopped

salt and freshly ground pepper

1   Preheat oven to 180°C.

2   Drizzle the parsnips, peppers and sweet potato (or a selection of root veg of your choice) with olive oil and season with salt and pepper and thyme. Put in a roasting tin in one layer and roast for about 30 mins until tender.

3   10 mins before the end, add a few sprigs of vine cherry tomatoes, with stalks still on.

4   Slice potatoes into 2cm-thick rounds.

5   Season and shallow fry on both sides in olive oil on medium heat until golden brown.

6   Transfer to a roasting tin and add vegetable stock to halfway up the side of the potato slices. Cover with foil and bake in oven at 170°C to cook through (approx. 15–20 mins).

7   Slice aubergine across into 1cm-thick rounds. Brush each slice with olive oil, sprinkle with polenta flour and fry in 1 tbsp olive oil until golden brown. Place in oven at 170°C to cook through (10 mins).

8   Warm the plates in the oven for a few minutes. Place the fondant potato in the middle with the aubergine slice on top and the roasted tomatoes on top of that to make a stack. Arrange roasted veg around the plate and garnish with chopped chives.

FRESH PASTA

SERVES 4 | PREP TIME: 10 MINS, PLUS 30 MINS RESTING TIME
COOKING TIME: 6 MINS

You will need a pasta machine for this – the hand crank sort or an attachment for a food mixer. Although it is possible to roll it out by hand, I've never done it!

225g 00 pasta flour

1 egg + 4 yolks

2 tsp of olive oil

½ tsp salt

4 tbsp polenta flour (or 00 pasta flour)

1 Mix the pasta flour, egg + yolks, olive oil and salt together for 3 mins in a food processor until it comes together into a ball. Allow to rest for 30 mins in the fridge, covered.

2 Cut into 4 pieces. Work with the first one and cover the others. Roll out using 1 tbsp of flour to prevent sticking.

3 Set up the pasta machine and pass the dough through the widest setting first, then thinner and thinner until you have reached setting number 5.

4 Cut pasta into shapes of your choice. The machine will have a cutting blade for this or you can use a knife and cut into squares. Dust shapes in a little flour to prevent sticking together.

5 Repeat steps 3 and 4 with the other 3 pieces of dough.

6 Bring a large pan of water to the boil. Add pasta, stir gently and boil on medium heat for about 6 mins. Take out a piece and see if it is cooked to your liking.

7 Drain and serve with Roasted Tomatoes with Garlic, Rosemary & Olive Oil (see p.114) and No Bones Jones Pesto (see p.128)

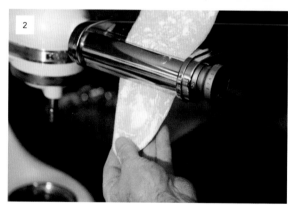

LEEK, MUSHROOM & CHESTNUT WELLINGTON

SERVES 4 | PREP TIME: 30 MINS, PLUS 20 MINS IN FRIDGE
COOKING TIME: 50 MINS–1 HOUR

This is a great centrepiece for Christmas Day or a dinner party. Serve with homemade Vegetarian Gravy (see p.128), cranberry sauce, roasted root vegetables and sprouts.

3 leeks – washed and chopped

3 sticks of celery – chopped

300g chestnut mushrooms – chopped

3 cloves of garlic – chopped

200g fresh spinach – chopped

3 tsp fresh rosemary or basil – chopped + sprig of rosemary for garnish

200g cream cheese

100g chestnuts or walnuts – chopped in half

zest of ½ a lemon

375g ready-rolled puff pastry

1 egg yolk

olive oil

salt and freshly ground black pepper

1 Preheat the oven to 190°C.

2 Fry the leeks, celery, mushrooms and garlic in 2 tbsp of olive oil over a medium heat until everything is quite soft (about 15 mins).

3 Add the spinach and rosemary/basil. Cook for a few moments, then take off the heat.

4 Add cream cheese, chestnuts/walnuts, lemon zest and a pinch of salt and a good grind of black pepper. Stir thoroughly and allow to cool.

5 When the mixture is cold, form it into a large sausage shape with the aid of cling-film (see photo 1). It will need to fit into the pastry.

6 Wrap it up and chill in the fridge (about 20 mins).

7 Unroll the pastry. Unwrap the sausage-shaped filling from the cling-film and place on top of the pastry (see photo 2).

8 Roll it up in the pastry, and paste the edges together using a pastry brush dipped in egg yolk. Place the joined edge underneath to make a neat shape. Close the ends together and brush all over with the egg yolk.

9 Make a few decorative slashes across the top to allow the steam to escape. Grind black pepper over the top.

10 Bake in oven for approx. 50 mins to 1 hour, until golden brown.

LENTIL & VEGETABLE STEW

VEGAN **GF** SERVES 4 | PREP TIME: 20 MINS | COOKING TIME: 40 MINS

This is my basic stew: nutritious and delicious, and lentils and pulses are a great source of fibre and protein. A versatile one-pot wonder which can be cooked over any heat source – camping or kitchen. Your kitchen or open campfire area will smell fabulous – such a small effort gives you a really wholesome meal. Of course you can add all manner of other veg to this – what needs using up in your fridge? If using green veg, don't overcook it – put it in 5–10 mins before the end. Serve with fresh bread, rice, quinoa or by itself.

1 large onion (or 2 leeks)
– peeled and sliced

3 carrots – peeled and chopped

3 sticks of celery – chopped

3 cloves of garlic – peeled and crushed

2 tbsp of vegetable oil

100g red lentils

1 x 400g tin of chopped tomatoes

1 tsp dried herbs – basil, thyme, rosemary or mixed herbs

1 rounded tsp salt and a good grind of black pepper

1 small handful of fresh coriander – chopped

1 In a large saucepan, heat the oil over a medium heat. Fry the onions/leeks, carrots, celery and garlic, stirring around from time to time, for 5 mins.

2 Add the lentils, tomatoes, dried herbs, salt and pepper and 350ml of boiling water. Stir thoroughly and bring to the boil, then turn down, cover and simmer for about 40 mins, until everything is tender.

3 Take off the heat. Just before serving, garnish with the coriander.

VARIATIONS

VEGGIE LASAGNE: Use this as the main filling.

VEGGIE COTTAGE PIE: Put it into a baking dish, cover with mashed or sliced boiled potatoes, sprinkle with cheese and bake in oven at 180°C until golden brown.

Or blend it into a smooth **SOUP**.

NUT & VEGETABLE ROAST

GF SERVES 4 | PREP TIME: 30 MINS | COOKING TIME: 45 MINS

This is just a basic framework for a nut roast – feel free to add extra veg, seeds or different cheese, such as feta. I also cook asparagus, leave it whole and layer it in the middle, which looks & tastes great. If you cut the leftovers into thick slices, toss in polenta flour and fry in a pan on both sides – *voilà*, you have veggie burgers!

---

3 carrots

1 large onion

3 sticks of celery

6 chestnut mushrooms

2 cloves of garlic

2 tbsp vegetable oil

150g cooked brown rice

225g mixed nuts (or seeds)

1 tsp GF vegetable stock powder – dissolve in 2 tbsp of hot water

2 tbsp tomato purée

1 heaped tsp of fresh rosemary – chopped small

100g fresh spinach – chopped

salt and freshly ground black pepper

2 eggs – beaten

125g cheddar cheese – grated

1 Preheat oven to 170°C.

2 Dice the carrots, onion, celery, mushrooms and garlic quite small. Gently fry in 2 tbsp of vegetable oil for 5 mins.

3 Place the fried veg, rice, nuts/seeds, vegetable stock, tomato purée, rosemary, spinach and a little salt and pepper in a food processor and pulse-blend – not too fine.

4 Pour everything into a bowl and add eggs and cheddar. Mix all ingredients together thoroughly.

5 Line a 2lb loaf tin with baking parchment. Spoon the mixture in, pack it down and bake for 45 mins.

PUERTO RICAN RED BEAN STEW

VEGAN **GF** SERVES 4 | PREP TIME: 15 MINS | COOKING TIME: 25 MINS

A quick, easy and delicious midweek supper. Serve with rice, quinoa or bulgur wheat. Of course, you can cook your own beans – as we do – instead of using canned. A cardinal sin in festival catering is to run out of food! This almost happened at The Big Green Gathering – this dish was born out of the few ingredients we had left, remembering a similar dish cooked by our lovely Puerto Rican friend Claire and her husband Dave in New York.

1 tbsp vegetable oil

1 onion – finely sliced

2 cloves of garlic – chopped

1 red chilli – chopped (or less/more, as you wish)

2 red peppers – de-seeded & sliced

1 rounded tsp dried oregano

100g block of creamed coconut

2 x 400g cans of chopped tomatoes

1 x 400g can of red kidney beans or cooked black-eyed beans

165g sweetcorn

salt and freshly ground black pepper

1   Heat oil in a saucepan and fry onion, garlic, chilli, oregano and red pepper for about 6–7 mins over medium heat, stirring from time to time.

2   Add coconut, turn down heat, cover and cook until the veg are soft (about 10 mins).

3   Add tomatoes, drained beans and sweetcorn. Cook for a further 10 mins. until everything is hot and bubbling. Season to taste.

SMOKED PAPRIKA & ROASTED CUMIN MOUSSAKA

GF SERVES 4 | PREP TIME: 30 MINS | COOKING TIME: 30 MIN

At the start of each season I choose two spices to work with. Smoked paprika and roasted cumin go hand in hand, complementing each other so well. It is great to bring new flavours onto the food stand.

MOUSSAKA

2 aubergines – thickly sliced

3 large potatoes – peeled and sliced

1 onion – chopped

vegetable oil

olive oil

1½ heaped tsp smoked paprika

3 heaped tsp ground cumin

3 garlic cloves – finely chopped

500g passata

salt and freshly ground black pepper

1 tsp sugar

CHEAT'S CHEESE SAUCE

200g cream cheese

4 tbsp milk

small handful of grated cheddar

small handful of diced feta

1   Preheat oven to 170°C.

2   Parboil potatoes (about 8 mins).

3   Brush each side of the aubergine slices with a little olive oil. Roast in the oven for 15 mins, turning over halfway through.

4   Heat a frying pan. Add ground cumin and dry roast for about 5 mins until you can smell the spice. Take off the heat.

5   Fry onion in 1 tbsp of vegetable oil over a medium heat for a 5–6 minutes until soft.

6   Add paprika and cumin and gently fry for another minute. Add passata and remove from heat.

7   In another pan, heat 2 tbsp of vegetable oil until hot. Add fresh garlic and take off the heat immediately to prevent the garlic burning.

8   Pour the garlic and oil into the onions and passata, and stir. Add salt and pepper to taste. Stir in sugar.

9   To make the cheese sauce, mash cream cheese and milk together with a fork, sprinkling in the grated cheese little by little.

10 In an ovenproof dish suitable for a lasagne, layer potatoes, tomato sauce and aubergines. Pour the cheese sauce over the dish, and dot with small cubes of feta.

11 Bake in the oven until golden and bubbling (about 30 mins).

STUFFED VEGETABLES

VEGAN **GF**   SERVES 4 | PREP TIME: 30 MINS | COOKING TIME: 50 MINS

So colourful, so delicious and so easy to feed a crowd. Use one vegetable per person, plus extra tomatoes. I like to save time by making extra and using that to start the next meal, so I suggest making too much of the Brown Rice & Green Lentils (see p.102) and then using it as your base stuffing for this recipe.

---

3 peppers

3 tomatoes

1 aubergine

300g mushrooms – sliced

3 cloves of garlic – chopped

2 cups Brown Rice & Green Lentils, or any cooked rice, quinoa or lentils

2 tbsp GF soya sauce

1 bunch fresh parsley – chopped (leaves only)

3 tbsp olive oil

salt and freshly ground black pepper

1   Preheat oven to 160°C.

2   Slice off the top 2cm of the peppers with stalk, keeping the cap for later. De-seed.

3   Slice off the stalk end of the tomatoes, again keeping the cap. Scrape out the soft part of the centre, without damaging outer skin. Keep the pulp to one side for later.

4   Cut aubergine in half from stalk end down. Scoop out the flesh from the centre and put to one side for later, leaving two boat shapes.

5   Fry sliced mushrooms and garlic in 1 tbsp olive oil for 5 mins over a medium heat, stirring from time to time.

6   Add tomato and aubergine flesh and cook for 5 mins.

7   Take off the heat. Add parsley, soya sauce and Brown Rice & Green Lentils mixture. Stir together.

8   Place hollowed out vegetables in a roasting tin and fill with stuffing mix from steps 5–7. Replace the vegetable caps. Pour boiling water into the bottom of the roasting tin around the vegetables, about 5cm deep.

9   Drizzle with 2 tbps olive oil and sprinkle with salt and freshly ground black pepper.

10 Cover tin with foil. Put in oven for 30 mins, then remove foil (be careful – it will be hot!) and cook for 20 mins more.

THAI CURRY WITH BUTTER BEANS, ASPARAGUS & SPINACH

VEGAN   GF   SERVES 4 | PREP TIME: 15 MINS | COOKING TIME: 20 MINS

Our boys love making this curry – once the paste is made, it's so easy, quick and tasty. Keep the paste in the fridge and make another curry with it within the week, or freeze it. You can change the veg in this recipe and make it with baby corn, broccoli and chickpeas.

CURRY PASTE

10 red chillies – de-stalked and halved

1 small onion – peeled and chopped

6 cloves of garlic – peeled

1 thumb-size piece of ginger – peeled and finely chopped

2 stalks of lemongrass – chopped

2 coriander plants – using stalks for this paste (you will need the leaves later – chopped)

10 black peppercorns

1 tsp ground coriander

1 tsp cumin seeds

1 tsp ground turmeric

4 tbsp GF soya sauce (or tamari)

1 tsp salt

2 tbsp vegetable oil

1 lime – zest & juice

2 tbsp soft brown sugar

1. To make the curry paste, blend all the curry paste ingredients together in a food processor till it forms a paste.

2. Fry 2 tbsp of curry paste (or more according to your taste for spiciness) gently in a saucepan for 5 mins, stirring.

3. Add coconut milk and butter beans. Stir thoroughly and bring to a gentle simmer. Cook for 10 mins.

4. Add asparagus/green beans and cook until veg is tender (about 6–8 mins). For the last 2 mins, add spinach and the chopped coriander leaves.

5. Check seasoning.

CURRY

1 x 400g can coconut milk

1 x 400g can butter beans – drained

150g asparagus or green beans – chopped

2 large handfuls of fresh spinach – chopped

salt and freshly ground pepper

DESSERTS

BAKED LEMON & VANILLA CHEESECAKE

GF PREP TIME: 30 MINS | COOKING TIME: 40 MINS

This recipe makes a large cheesecake – our favourite. Eaten in the winter, it reminds me of summer. This is a much lighter version of a traditional baked cheesecake. Serve with fresh fruit such as raspberries.

175g GF (or non-GF if you prefer) digestive or ginger biscuits

60g butter + a little extra for greasing cake tin

600g full-fat cream cheese

175g caster sugar

6 eggs – separate whites and yolks

1 lemon – zest & juice

2 tsp vanilla extract

100g Greek yogurt

100g fresh fruit (your choice)

1 tsp icing sugar – sieved

1. Preheat oven to 150°C.

2. Crush the biscuits – the easiest way to do this is in a food processor.

3. Use a little butter to grease the inside of a round, loose-bottom cake tin, 24cm across.

4. In a saucepan, melt 60g butter over a low heat and then add the biscuit crumbs. Mix together thoroughly and tip into cake tin. Press down firmly to create the base.

5. In a mixing bowl, beat together the cream cheese, caster sugar, egg yolks, lemon zest and juice, vanilla extract and Greek yogurt.

6. Whisk egg whites in a clean bowl until stiff, then gently fold into the cream-cheese mixture. Pour into the cake tin on top of the biscuit base. Bake in the oven for 40 mins until set.

7. Switch off the oven, open the oven door and allow the cheesecake to cool. This should prevent the top of the cheesecake from cracking. Only put it in the fridge once it is completely cold.

8. Dust with icing sugar and serve with fresh fruit of your choice.

BANANA GATEAU

PREP TIME: 30 MINS | COOKING TIME: 30 MINS

So, so good. Children love this as a change from chocolate cake. This recipe was given to Jill while she was working in New Zealand – it was a family recipe from her friend Maura.

200g soft brown sugar

140g butter – soft

4 ripe bananas

80ml natural yogurt

2 tsp vanilla extract

2 large eggs

230g plain flour

1 tsp bicarbonate of soda

½ tsp baking powder

300ml double cream

1tbsp icing sugar

a little lemon juice

a little chocolate for decoration

1 Preheat oven to 170°C.

2 Cream together brown sugar and butter in a small mixing bowl until fluffy.

3 In a second bowl, mash 3 bananas and then beat together with the yogurt, vanilla extract and eggs.

4 Sieve the flour, bicarbonate of soda and baking powder into a third bowl.

5 Mix the contents of all three bowls together and stir thoroughly.

6 Line two 20cm sponge tins with baking parchment. Pour the batter in and bake for approx. 30 mins. Then leave until cool.

7 Whip the double cream with 1 tbsp of icing sugar. Spread half on top of one of the cakes. Slice the last banana and sprinkle it with lemon juice to prevent it turning brown, then add this on top of the cream before sandwiching the two halves together.

8 Cover the top of the cake with the other half of the whipped cream, and sprinkle shavings of chocolate across the cake to decorate.

CHOCOLATE FUDGE CAKE

VEGAN   PREP TIME: 20 MINS | COOKING TIME: 30 MINS

This was our children's birthday cake for many years, made into a castle or dinosaur island or whatever they were into at the time!

CAKE

250g self-raising flour

3 rounded tbsp cocoa

½ tsp salt

1 rounded tsp bicarbonate of soda

170g soft brown sugar

3 tbsp golden syrup

240ml plant-based milk – soya, oat, etc

120ml vegetable oil

1 tsp vanilla extract

VEGAN CHOCOLATE GANACHE ICING

250g dark chocolate of your choice

250ml soya or coconut cream

1 Preheat oven to 170°C.

2 Sift the flour, cocoa, salt and bicarbonate of soda together.

3 Add sugar, golden syrup, milk, oil and vanilla extract.

4 Whisk all the ingredients together until well blended.

5 Line two 20cm cake tins with baking parchment.

6 Pour half the mixture into each tin and bake at 170°C for 25–30 mins.

7 Take out of the tins and allow to cool for about 40 mins, until cool to the touch.

8 Melt the vegan chocolate ganache icing ingredients together gently in a saucepan over a low heat, then allow to cool.

9 Use the ganache icing to sandwich the cake together and decorate the top.

GRANNY JONES' STICKY TOFFEE BREAD & BUTTER PUDDING

PREP TIME: 30 MINS | COOKING TIME: 40 MINS

A favourite on the festival circuit, when ankle-deep in mud – to keep you going late into the night! Even people who hate conventional bread and butter pudding love this. Not healthy, but filling and yummy! Serve with Greek yoghurt, ice cream or cream. My granny may be dead and gone, but her pud lives on!

BREAD & BUTTER PUDDING

1 small loaf of white unsliced bread (doesn't work so well with brown)

80g butter + a little extra for greasing baking dish

50g raisins or dried fruit of your choice

5 large eggs

700ml whole milk

100g soft brown sugar + a little extra to sprinkle on top

STICKY TOFFEE SAUCE

65g caster sugar

65g butter

80g soft brown sugar

125ml golden syrup

150ml single cream

1. Preheat oven to 160°C.

2. Butter a deep-sided baking dish (approx. 30cm x 25cm).

3. Cut the bread into chunks, about 5cm x 3cm. Butter pieces randomly to use up all butter.

4. Place in the baking dish and sprinkle with dried fruit.

5. Crack eggs into a large bowl and whisk with a fork to break up the yolks. Add the milk and most of the sugar and mix together.

6. Pour over the bread, pressing down the chunks to absorb the liquid, and then sprinkle with a little sugar. Leave for 10 mins then bake in the oven for approx. 40 mins, until golden and set in the middle.

7. To make the sticky toffee sauce, place the caster sugar, brown sugar, butter and syrup in a saucepan over a medium/low heat. Melt everything together, stirring until smooth. Bring to the boil for 3 mins.

8. Take off the heat and add the cream. Be careful: it will bubble and spit!

9. When you take the pudding out of the oven, check it is cooked by poking a knife into the centre of the pudding to make sure the egg mixture is not runny. (Put it back in if it is!)

10. Pour some sauce over the cooked pudding and serve some more with it.

JILL'S EASY APPLE CAKE

PREP TIME: 30 MINS | COOKING TIME: 45 MINS

This reminds me so much of cakes I ate in Narayan's Pie Shop in Kathmandu. I often substitute apples with other fruit – pears & a handful of pecans, bananas with choc chips, pineapple with stem ginger & lime zest. It's a large, very versatile cake which freezes well. We often serve this with Granny Jones' Sticky Toffee sauce (see p.164).

---

4 large cooking apples – peeled, cored and sliced

juice of ½ a lemon

225g soft brown sugar

225g butter or margarine – soft

4 eggs – beaten

350g self-raising flour

2 level tsp of baking powder

1 level tsp ground cinnamon (optional)

1 Preheat oven to 170°C.

2 Sprinkle the lemon juice onto the apples.

3 Beat the sugar (reserving 2 tbsp to sprinkle on top later) and butter/margarine together for 5 mins.

4 Sieve the baking powder into the flour. Then add the flour and eggs (in two lots) into the mixture from step 3. Mix gently but thoroughly to make a soft cake batter.

5 Mix apples into cake batter, reserving 2 handfuls to decorate the top.

6 Line a large cake tin approx. 25cm across by 5cm deep with baking parchment.

7 Pour in the cake mixture. Decorate the top with the reserved apple, and sprinkle with soft brown sugar. You can also sprinkle with cinnamon (optional).

8 Bake for about 45 mins.

9 To check it is cooked through, pierce the centre of the cake with a cocktail stick. If it comes out clean, it's cooked.

LEMON CUP WITH CARDAMOM SHORTBREAD

SERVES: 8 | PREP TIME: 40 MINS | COOKING TIME: 30 MINS

Make in advance, in the morning or even one day before you wish to serve them. My favourite pud for many years. I use 8 small ovenproof coffee cups (ideally with matching saucers to serve) to cook the pudding in.

CARDAMOM SHORTBREAD

150g plain flour

25g cornflour

25g polenta or rice flour

50g caster sugar

100g butter – soft but not melted

10 green cardamom pods – discard pods and grind seeds with the back of a teaspoon, or use 1 tsp ground cardamom

LEMON CUPS

juice of 3 large lemons

4 large eggs

300ml double cream

200g caster sugar

1. Preheat oven to 170°C.

2. Mix all shortbread ingredients together until thoroughly combined to form a dough.

3. Lightly flour a clean worksurface or table. Tip the mixture out on to it and roll out to about twice the thickness of a £1 coin. (It is quite crumbly but persevere – this means it will be a delicious biscuit!)

4. Cut or stamp out small biscuits, pricking each one twice with a fork. Place on a baking tray and bake for 8–10 mins until golden brown. NB Take a look at them after 8 mins as they burn easily. Take out of the oven and leave to cool.

5. Turn oven down to 140°C. Boil kettle ready for *bain marie*.

6. Place all lemon cup ingredients together in a mixing bowl and whisk until smooth.

7. Place ovenproof cups in a roasting tin. Pour lemon mixture into cups and boiling water into a roasting tin around them to create a *bain marie*. NB For safety have everything by the oven with baking tin on oven shelf before pouring in the water.

8. Cook for 20 mins. Take cups out of water after removing from oven, to prevent further cooking.

9. Serve cup on matching saucer, with biscuit on the side.

LEMON POLENTA & RASPBERRY CAKE

GF PREP TIME: 30 MINS | COOKING TIME: 45 MINS

Of all the delicious cakes that Jill makes, this is my absolute favourite of all time. At 10.30 a.m. during a festival I take a few moments to sit and relax, with a coffee in hand and a slice of heaven! The texture and flavours are outstanding.

CAKE

210g butter – soft

225g caster sugar

3 eggs – beaten

zest of 2 lemons – finely grated

juice of 1 lemon

115g polenta

115g gluten-free self-raising flour

1 tsp baking powder

100g fresh raspberries

LEMON DRIZZLE ICING

juice of 1 lemon

3 tbsp of icing sugar – sieved

1   Preheat oven to 160°C.

2   Cream the butter and caster sugar together.

3   Add eggs, lemon zest (from both lemons) and juice (from one lemon only), polenta, flour and baking powder. Mix everything together thoroughly.

4   Line a round or square 23cm cake tin with baking parchment.

5   Pour in the cake mixture and push the raspberries lightly and randomly into the mixture.

6   Bake for approx. 40–45 mins.

7   Stir together the lemon drizzle icing ingredients in a small bowl. Pour over the cooked cake when it is still warm.

SUMMER PORRIDGE

VEGAN PREP TIME: 10 MINS | COOKING TIME: NONE

First discovered by Jill when she worked at Hotel Alpina in Luzern in Switzerland in the late 1970s. It has evolved over the years, and these days we use plant milk.

250g jumbo oats

oat milk, or any other plant milk of your choice

50g sunflower seeds

25g pumpkin seeds

50g cashew nuts & pecan nuts

100g dried fruit – cranberries, apricots, sour cherries, sultanas, etc.

chopped fresh fruit – I normally use 1 apple & 1 banana, but mango, blueberries, raspberries or any soft fruit you like would work too.

a little date syrup or soft brown sugar to sweeten

1 Mix the oats, seeds, nuts and dried fruit all together.

2 Add enough plant-based milk to just cover. Leave overnight in the fridge.

3 The next day, add the chopped fresh fruit.

4 As this is not very sweet, add date syrup or brown sugar to your taste.

Also from Y Lolfa:

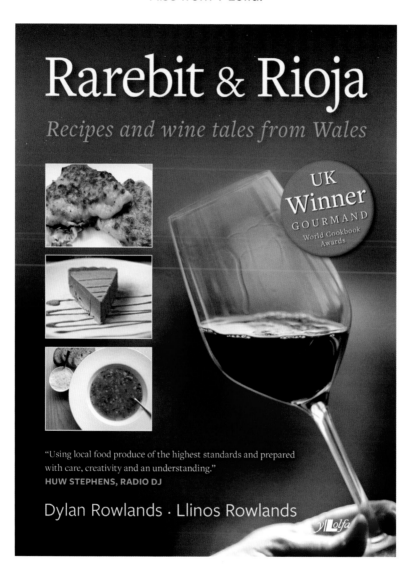

£14.99